3-D Explosion:
Simply FABULOUS Art Quilt Illusions

By Cara Gulati

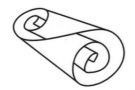

Published by
Doodle Press
PO Box 508
Nicasio, CA 94946
www.doodlepress.com

Dedication
To my husband Dhruv and our furry four legged family including Sammy, Rosie, and The Pud. Thank you for cooking lots of dinners and for your love, attention, and support.

To my parents Hank and Cathy Feenstra. Thank you for raising me to believe I could do anything and to just go for it.

Acknowledgements
I want to thank my friends/editors who helped me make this book a reality:
Val Manning, Laura Callahan, Joanne Farrell, and Laura Nownes. Without you I would still be editing and there would not be enough commas.

To my friends Pat Dicker, Julie Hirota, Carol Larsen, and the Threadheads, thank you for your constant encouragement.

And for my friends who have been along for the ride, Karen Boutte and Beth Ferrier, climbing the ladder and riding the slide with you both has been a blast.

To the shop owners who helped me start my teaching career and keep me going, thank you to Susie Ernst of the Quilted Angel in Petaluma, Sally Davies and Sharona Fishrup of New Pieces in Berkeley, Diane Massy-Todd and Nancy Eberlin of Quiltmaker in Napa, Jennifer McCoy of Pumpkinseed Quilts and Textiles in San Rafael, and Carolie Hensley of the Cotton Patch in Lafayette.

Text, art work and photos of how-to photography © 2004 Cara Gulati
Photographs of quilts © 2004 by Gregory Case, www.gregorycase.com.
except where noted

Publisher: Doodle Press
Printed in Ohio by Tri-State Printing Company
First Printing 2004

Front Cover: Colossal Scrolls
Back Cover: Rosie's Rainbow Flower

Teachers: Look for teaching tips at www.doodlepress.com

Every effort was made to give you accurate information. Your results will vary with fabric, thread choices and sewing skills. No guarantee is given or implied.

Library of Congress number 2001097789

ISBN: 0-9761626-0-1

Contents

Introduction: The Happy Accident

I came upon this 3-D Explosion design idea while playing with curved lines. After drawing lots of nice curves I just knew something simple was needed in order to create something really spectacular. So I added perspective points and lines to the curved drawings. It was so exciting that I kept creating more and more of these drawings and then one was just right. So I made the Colossal Scrolls quilt up in fabric and it was even more exciting than I ever expected! That was just the beginning. I have been teaching this technique nationally and now these 3-D Explosion inspired designs are appearing in quilt shows all over the country.

You, too, can create your own fabulous art quilt design. It's a very simple recipe. And since recipes are just guidelines, sometimes they need to be changed to suit your own tastes. Remember, more is better whether it's more fabric choices or thread colors. More is just more interesting!

This book will teach you how to create your own 3-D Explosion design from drawing, choosing fabrics, blowing it up, and sewing the top together. I will also give you tips on quilting the designs.

Supplies for Starting your 3-D Explosion

Sewing machine with adjustable zig zag capabilities. Extra credit for an extension table.
Drawing pad: 18" X 24" is best
Sharp pencils
Sharpie pen, thin
Freezer paper
Masking tape
Water-soluble glue stick
Scissors for paper and fabric
Open-Toe sewing machine foot
Invisible thread: Clear monofilament polyester thread
Light box
Design Wall, something you can pin into
Pins
Thread to match your fabrics for quilting
Fabric: How much you need will be determined by your project and will include gradation sets of fabric and one or more striped fabrics, background fabric (best auditioned before purchased), batting and backing and binding.

If you choose to design your art quilt, there is no formula for the exact amount of design fabric, background fabric, thread, batting and backing you will need. It all depends upon the size of your project. I recommend that you decide on the finished size of your design before you try to figure out about how much fabric you will need for your project. I say "about" because you will need to cut out odd-shaped pieces from your fabrics. You will also want extra fabric in case you change your mind and need to cut something out more than once. Your fabrics will take on the characteristic of Swiss cheese when you are finished with them. I suggest you bring crackers!

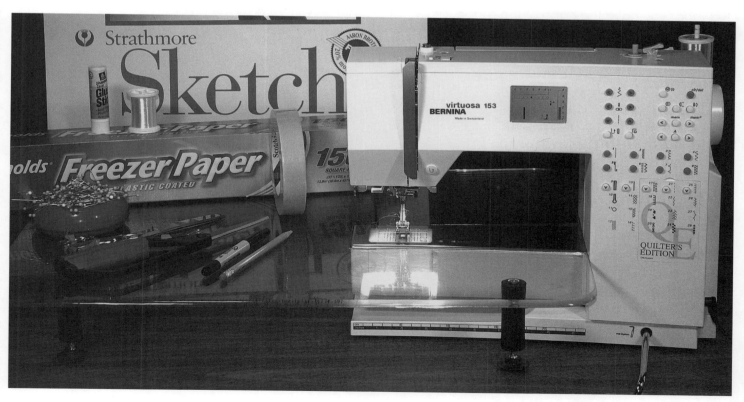

3-D Explosion

A Pencil and a Ruler can be a Girl's Best Friends
(the secret to drawing the design is revealed)

I can hear you right now. "Draw it? No way! I can't draw!" You can draw an "S" shape, right? I bet you can also draw a straight line along the edge of a ruler. That is all it takes. Really!

Let's go! Draw an "S" shape with some extra curly lines at the beginning and end of the line, something like these:

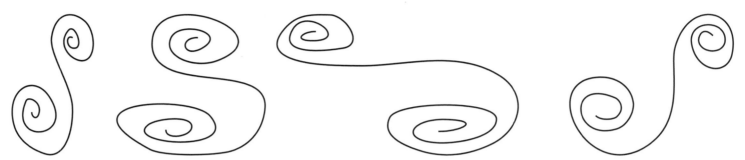

Practice drawing these shapes to loosen up your arm and hand. Relax and remember:
- You can't do it wrong.
- Bigger is better when it comes to the size of your scroll shape.
- Try to resist the urge to erase anything, because you will get really good at erasing and not as good at creating your line with one fluid movement. Anything you can draw with one line will always look more natural than a line you started, stopped and started again.
- And the more drawings you make, the better your lines will become. Not only that, but you will begin to get shapes that you like.

Now that you have the hang of the shape, draw ten "S" shapes with one shape on each 18" X 24" page. Fill up most of the page with your shape.

After that is done, grab the first "S" drawing and put a point somewhere on your page outside of your "S" shape and near the edge of your paper.

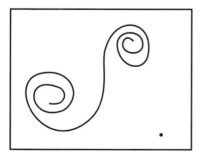

This point will be known as your perspective point. It sounds technical, but it's really only a dot on the paper. The secret to the design is how your lines get from the "S" shape to the perspective point!

Now you will need your straight edge. Place your pencil on the dot and line up the straight edge with the first edge of the curve it meets on the left side. See how the curve swerves towards and away from the straight edge, just meeting it at one point. Now draw a line starting from the edge of the curve where it meets the straight edge to the dot and stop.

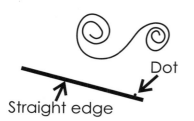

Dot

Straight edge

Line up straight edge with edge of curve and dot

Draw your line

Putting your pencil back on the dot, slide your ruler over to the right until it lines up with the edge of another curved line. TIP: <u>STRAIGHT PERSPECTIVE LINES NEVER CROSS OVER CURVED LINES.</u> Check to see if there is another curved line in between the edge of the curve that lines up with the ruler and the perspective point. If there is, start the line at the curved edge and stop it right at the curved line that crosses your straight edge. Don't continue the line to the point. See how mine stops.

Line up the straight edge with the edge of the next curve and the dot

Draw your line down to the next curved line and stop

Lines that disappear behind other curved lines are the secret to the illusion. The rule is simple, so how about we make it our mantra? Repeat out loud: <u>STRAIGHT PERSPECTIVE LINES NEVER CROSS OVER CURVED LINES.</u> Excellent!

Put your pencil back on the dot and slide your straight edge over to the right until it meets the edge of another curved line and draw another straight line in the direction of your dot. Repeat this process until you have drawn every straight line you need to finish creating the design. Every edge of your "S" shaped curve line should have a straight line going in the direction of your perspective point. Most of them will stop at another curved line. If your drawing looks funny, you might be missing a line or it may be drawn upwards from the curve instead of in the direction of your point. Run your straight edge through your drawing again and check your lines.

Go to the next page to see my drawing as I add each line.

3-D Explosion

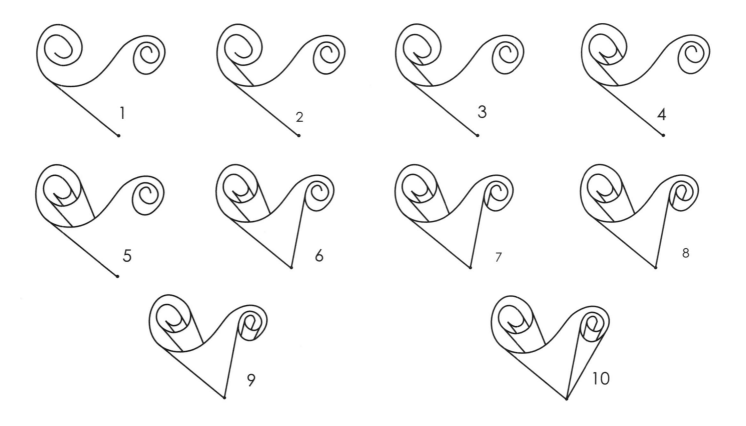

Finish adding perspective points and lines to the rest of the ten drawings you made with the "S" shapes. Put your point in different places on the page. Here are some examples of what simply fabulous things that can happen when you try different perspective points:

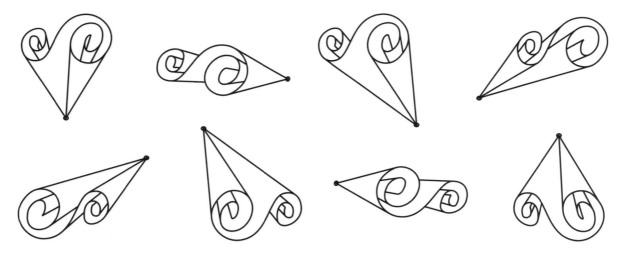

TIP: <u>THE SHAPE OF THE DRAWING PAPER HAS NO BEARING ON THE FINAL SHAPE OF YOUR QUILT.</u> These fun shapes you are creating will be appliquéd to a background later on. Try to look at the paper as just a work space and not the shape of your finished quilt. You will get to audition backgrounds and you don't have to make that decision until much later!

3-D Explosion

In the meantime, your simple scroll design may not be as fabulous as you think it should be. I have a few tricks up my sleeve so stay with me. You have the basics so let me show you how to add some excitement.

Choose one of your drawings. Let's add a second scroll, but only a half. This is cool because you only need to draw half of an "S" shape! Somewhere on the outside of your completed scroll shape draw a half scroll and have the line end at the curved line of your completed scroll. Check out this illustration:

Now let's add the straight lines, one at a time, remembering our mantra: <u>STRAIGHT PERSPECTIVE LINES NEVER CROSS OVER CURVED LINES.</u>

Isn't this fun? You can draw some new designs with this half scroll added to your design or you could add half scrolls to the designs you already have.

This is how the Simple Sammy Scroll project came to be. You can use one of your own drawings and make it into a finished quilt. Or, you can go beyond that. Do I hear you asking me how? Oh boy, this is where it gets really exciting! You can take the design and repeat it once:

1 repeat

3-D Explosion

You can repeat it three times for a total of four motifs:

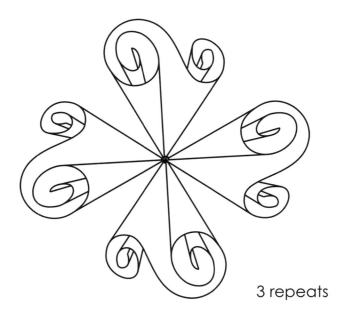

3 repeats

Now that's fabulous! Here is another idea. Let's mirror the basic shape. Mirroring means that you will take your drawing, repeat it and then reverse it. It might look something like this:

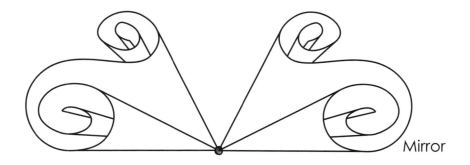

Mirror

3-D Explosion

You could mirror again, taking your mirrored design and mirroring it as a unit. That means you will make two right side facing designs and two other-side facing designs and set them in opposite corners. It might look something like this:

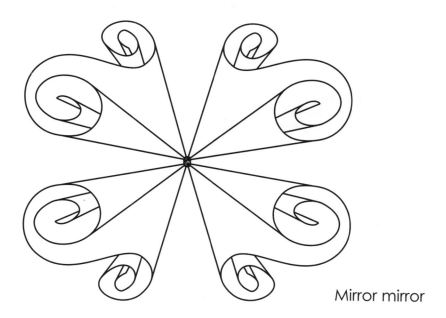

Mirror mirror

This could go on forever! Maybe you are interested in something more organic in nature, something a bit less predictable. Something like the last project in this book called Colossal Scrolls. The quilt is on the front of the book as well and it's probably the reason you picked it up in the first place. These are my favorite kinds of designs! Here is how you make them:

Draw a few "S" shapes on your 18" X 24" paper.

Next mark a perspective point. Draw your lines in the direction of the perspective point, keeping our mantra in mind: <u>STRAIGHT PERSPECTIVE LINES NEVER CROSS OVER CURVED LINES.</u>

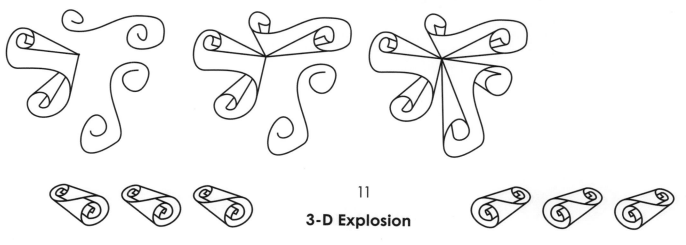

3-D Explosion

Isn't this fun? Now the secret has been revealed and you can draw all kinds of cool exploding shapes! Take a look at the Colossal Scrolls quilt to see this type of designing with "S" shapes all over the place. Try something like that on paper and see how you like it.

Maybe this method is a little scary or too uncontrolled for you. In that case another solution to that is to take a few of your simple scroll drawings and put them together in the same drawing, with their perspective points all meeting in the center. You still get a random look, but it will be a bit more manageable when you go to sew it together.

I would like to encourage you not to stop at your first drawing. You will find that as you draw more of these shapes, your curved lines will become more attractive and your scrolls will become more fabulous. Save your drawings after you are done. If you decide to make another exploding design, you will find your drawings to be quite inspiring.

On to Size!

3-D Explosion

3-D Explosion

Blowing Your Design Up!
(to the finished size and transferring on to freezer paper)

Now you have a pile of fabulous drawings. It's time to choose one and make it in fabric. First things first though. This part is not the most exciting part of the process, but it's like getting ready to paint a room. You have to do all the prep work like taping and laying tarps. If you don't do it, you will end up cleaning up paint spills and that will take twice as long, right?

There are three different options for making a larger drawing.

Option 1: You can tape together four or more sheets of paper from your drawing pad together to make a larger drawing surface and then draw a larger drawing. This can be scary, so I suggest that if you dislike this idea, try one either going to the copy store, or using an overhead projector.

Option 2: Take your drawing to a copy store that makes enlargements of the architectural variety. Try 200%, 300% and even 400% and see what you think. Go home, put them up on your wall and see which size makes you happy. You can still change your mind and choose to go larger, or somewhere in the middle and have another enlargement made.

Once your master drawing is the size you want, write "Right Side" on the printed side of the drawing. Now you will need to turn it over and use a Sharpie to trace the drawing on the back side of the paper. Once that is completed, write "Wrong Side" on the back of the drawing, outside of your design. (I will tell you why when we talk about freezer paper.)

Option 3: To use an overhead projector. Reduce the size of your drawing to 8" x 10 ½" or less. A copy store can do this for you. Then have them copy the design onto a piece of 8 ½" X 11" acetate. Write "Right Side" onto the right side of the drawing on the acetate with a permanent marker. This is the side that looks exactly the same as your drawing. This is an important step. On the reverse, write "Wrong Side" on the acetate.

Set up the overhead projector to face your design board or an empty wall. Plug it in and turn it on. Place your acetate on top of the glass with the words "Wrong Side" facing up at you and so that you can read them correctly on the wall. (I will tell you why when we talk about freezer paper.) Move the projector back and forth until you get the size of your design that you want. I enjoy this part of the process because I have complete control over how large or small I want my design to be.

I strongly suggest that you trace your design on to regular paper (not freezer paper) so that you have a master drawing. If you intend to repeat or mirror your drawing, it will be essential to have this master drawing. Draw it in PENCIL first. Then turn off the projector and trace it with a Sharpie. Write "Wrong Side" on your paper. If you will be mirroring your drawing, you will also need to trace the other side of your paper and write "Right Side" on it.

A few words about size. It has been overheard in my workshops that I was right after all. Bigger is better, easier to sew together and so much more exciting!

If you want to determine exactly how large you want your scroll design to be, measure your scroll and then divide that measurement onto your desired size. For example, if the longest side of your design is 16" and you want it to be 66", then 66 divided by 16% = 412.5%. 412.5% is how much larger you need to make your drawing of your scroll. To check your math, multiply 16 by 412.5% and you come up with 66". Now you can take your width and multiply it by 412.5% to get your new width.

Freezer Paper
Who says meat gets to have all the fun? I bet the people who make this stuff are laughing all the way to the bank. Who knew quilters would discover this as a tool in addition to use as a food wrapper?

3-D Explosion

Now it's time to explain the "Right Side" and "Wrong Side" labels. We want the right side of our fabric on our design wall to face out towards us. The freezer paper makes great templates because we can iron the smooth shiny side to the wrong side of the fabric. This means that the freezer paper has to be on the design wall with the shiny side facing towards out towards us.

With me so far? It's difficult to draw lines on the smooth shiny side of the freezer paper. So we trace the design onto the rough back side of the freezer paper, which means the tracing of our design must be the exact opposite of our drawing. It would be the "Wrong Side".

So what you want to do is to lay your master drawing on the table with the "Wrong Side" up. Lay the freezer paper on top of it with the rough side of the freezer paper on top. (If you need to join sheets of freezer paper together to make a larger piece, butt up the long edges and use one long piece of masking tape on the rough side of the paper to hold them together. It's much easier to ask for help from someone else than to do it yourself if your design is larger than you are.) Trace your design with a <u>PENCIL</u> onto the <u>ROUGH</u> side of the freezer paper. Use your straight edge for the straight lines.

Marking: This is the home stretch of the preparation! Once your design is traced onto the freezer paper in PENCIL, it's time to create some markings to help you sew your design together. I am going to use the Simple Sammy Scroll project design as our guide.

Step 1: Create some heavy registration marks. Remember your straight lines that stopped at the curved lines? Now we want to extend them with a nice heavy pencil mark beyond the curved line about 1". This will help with lining up the seams later on.

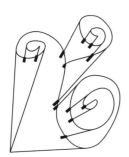

Step 2: Extend the lines of "S" shapes you drew. When you look at the center of your scroll shapes, you will see what I call a half moon or a comma shape. Mark another heavy, straight line to extend the end of the curved line.

Step 3: Make heavy registration marks across any straight lines that are long. It is only necessary to do this for the lines inside the design.

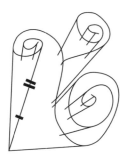

Step 4: Make heavy registration marks across the points inside the design.

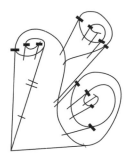

3-D Explosion

Step 5: Label the sewing order. Now you will learn to see your design as a bunch of different shapes that fit together. I like to give them names because it helps you to see the shapes when I talk about them. Let's do this visually.

Here is the shape of a basic scroll.

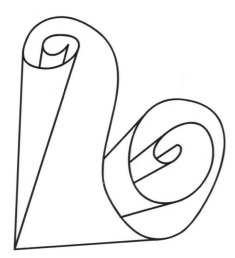

When you separate the templates, they look like this.

Notice how there are some shapes that look like cups or a cone.

Notice how there are some shapes that look like a horseshoe.

The center shapes are either a comma or a half moon. Notice how these shapes only have one straight line, not two like the cups, cones and horseshoes. These shapes are always #1 in the sewing order.

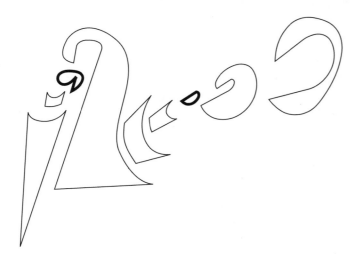

There is one more shape which looks like a slide. Not all complete scrolls will have this shape, but most do. I call it the "Show" piece because it's the largest piece.

Now that we have named the basic shapes of the scroll, we need to look at how they sew together. The first piece in the sewing order is always the comma or the half moon because these pieces have only one straight side instead of two straight sides. The next piece in the sewing order is going to be the template that shares that straight line with the comma or half moon.

Let's start with the side of the scroll with the half moon and label the half moon #1. It shares its straight line with a horseshoe shape that we will label #2.

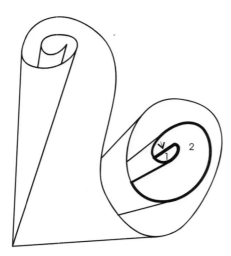

Look at the other straight line on the #2 shape and see that it joins up with a cup shape, which becomes #3.

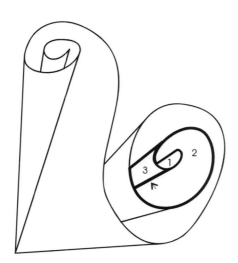

3-D Explosion

The other straight line in the cup shape joins another horseshoe shape which becomes #4.

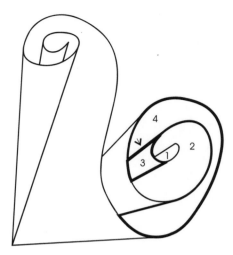

Now take your eye around the inside of the horseshoe shape until you come to the other straight line and you see it joins to another larger cup shape which becomes #5.

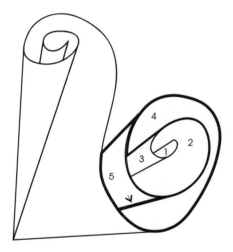

Notice how the other straight edge of the cup shape is the outside edge of your drawing. That means we are done with that half of the scroll.

3-D Explosion

Let's look at the comma piece in the other side of the scroll. Remember it is going to be the first piece on this side of the scroll because it has only one straight edge. We will label it #6 because it's the next piece we will pick up. The comma shares it's one straight line with a cup shape, which we will call #7.

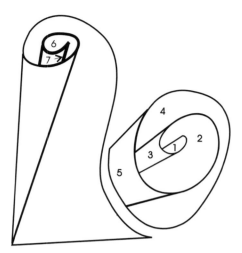

As we look at the other straight edge of #7, we see that it sews to our slide-shaped piece. Don't worry, it's not as hard as you may think. The slide becomes #8.

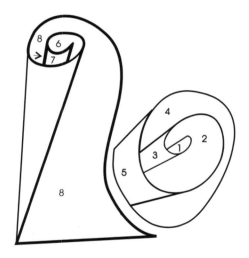

Almost done. Our slide has one more straight edge and it's a long one. It shares a straight edge with the cone shape, which becomes #9.

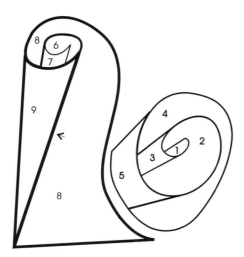

Last of all we need to label our templates with stripe and solid designations.

I have devised a great formula for making these scrolls appear to be 3-D. Think of each scroll shape as a piece of paper. One side of the paper has a striped pattern and the other side is a solid color. As you roll up the paper, the stripes change direction. And as the light hits the solid color, some areas are lighter and others darker. I have taken that and simplified it so that you can create the 3-D illusion easily.

Let's look at the illustration again. If I add stripes to one side of the scroll and change the direction of the stripes in each template, see how the illusion begins to come to life!

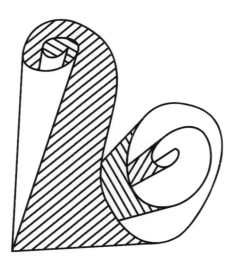

Now if I add some gradations (lights and darks) of grey to the "other side" of the scroll, it really looks like something that is rolled up.

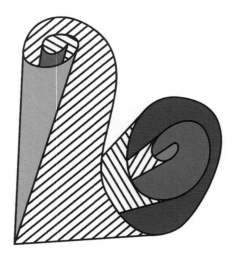

Take a look at the color photographs in the back of the book and look at them with new eyes. See how the fabrics are chosen to create the illusions. Are you inspired? I hope so!

Before we discuss fabric, let's do the last bit of labeling on our freezer paper templates.

First you need to label your templates with the words "Stripe" or "Solid". The solid label is for the areas that will have the gradations, which is explained in detail below. For now, we will just call them solid.

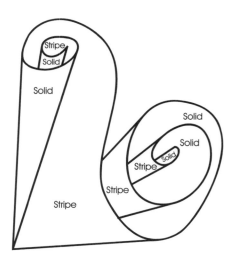

Take a look at the diagram above. Notice how your "Slide" template has a stripe. It helps your eye to see the illusion. Your stripe is your show fabric so let's show it off on the biggest template! Now let your eye follow the scroll around to see how it changes from stripes to solids as it rolls up on each side. Look at the Simple Sammy Scroll in color to help you see it even better. Label your freezer paper in the same manner.

If you are having a tough time "seeing" the design to label the stripes and solids, there is a another simple way to figure it out. Notice how the "Slide" is one piece that combines a cone shape and a horseshoe shape together. All the horseshoe and comma shapes underneath the stripe horseshoe side of the slide are stripes and the cups and cones on that same side are solids. On the other side of the scroll, all the cup shapes on the striped cup shape side are all stripes, and the horseshoes and commas on that side are all solids.

Horseshoe side

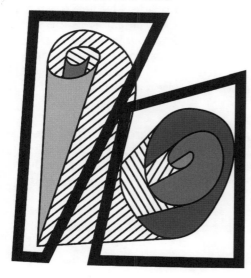

Cup Side

Next we need to choose the direction of the stripes. It's important that the stripes change direction to lead the eye around the design. I have found that the more obvious the change in the direction of the stripe from template to template, the more striking the design. It doesn't have to be realistic to create the 3-D illusion.

Let's start with the slide template. I like to have the stripe start at the corner and shoot out into the middle about half way between the two outside lines that meet at the point. I just use three lines to indicate which direction the stripes will go. Now you can add the same lines inside the other stripe template shapes and change the direction of the stripes. Here is what I did with mine:

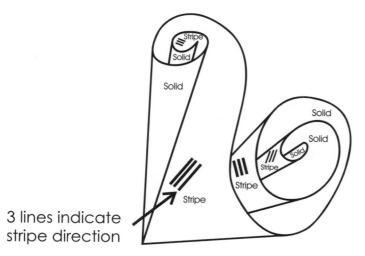

3 lines indicate
stripe direction

Now you have marked up your templates and established a sewing order. There is one more marking to add. It's a 3-Dot marking to indicate which straight edges you will need to glue under before you sew. It's best to talk about that while teaching you the sewing method. You will find this information in Simple Sammy Scroll project in detail. The boring part is over! Don't cut your templates apart yet. Onto fabric we go!

3-D Explosion

Stripes are not only for Men's Shirts!
(choosing fabrics for your project and why some are better than others)

I think this is most people's favorite part of making quilts: choosing the fabrics! I know it's mine.

Let's talk about fabric. More is better in my book. Pick a striped fabric you really like. It's best to chose a stripe with very straight lines. Wavy striped lines don't have the same eye-catching effect as the straight striped lines do. For example, look at the color photo of the Simple Sammy Scroll in the back of the book. Notice the nice straight rainbow stripe on the larger complete scroll. It's pretty obvious when it changes direction as the scroll rolls up. Now look at the half scroll with the black/rainbow stripe. It's not quite as noticeable that the stripe direction changes. The reason the black/rainbow stripe works is because your eye sees the big scroll shape first and understands what that shape is, so it then applies that knowledge to the half scroll and assumes it's the same type of shape. It's like the idea that the eye sees a complete circle even when it's not a closed shape.

Now that you have chosen a stripe, we need to talk about color before you chose your gradations for the "other side" of your scroll. The easiest gradation to understand is a color group that includes pastels and shades of one color. There are people who hand dye fabrics and package them this way. Using a prepared color gradation set makes it a no-brainer for the gradation side of the your scroll and might even start you on a new trend of collecting these sets.

The designation of light, medium and dark are all relative to what the fabric is next to. Hold up a green fabric and depending on what other green fabric you put it next to, it becomes either darker or lighter. It doesn't have to be a pastel to be "light," or have lots of black in it to be "dark."

Colors can also gradate from one color to another, say red to yellow. Hand dyers do it best by changing the amounts of each color in the dye pot for each step in the group. So your gradation set would have reds, red/oranges, oranges, yellow/oranges and yellows. These groups work well for your gradation sets too.

People want to pick colors that play together nicely when they choose fabrics for a quilt design. We want to do the opposite for this project. Success comes with contrast! Your quilt design will be more successful if you choose gradations in colors that are not in your striped fabric. Then your seam lines will appear nice and sharp. If your colors blend, seam lines and design lines become confusing and your eye may not pick up the design.

I also find that opposites on the color wheel really pop. For instance, if you have a red stripe and your gradations are shades of green, your scroll will be very eye-catching. If your stripes are red and your gradations are shades of orange, which is right next to red on the color wheel, it will look nice, but it won't pop as much as the red-green combination. The basic opposites on the color wheel are: RED and GREEN, BLUE and ORANGE, and YELLOW and PURPLE.

Now that being said, these are guidelines that I find provide maximum impact. Guidelines are like recipes. You can add more chocolate and make it taste better. So if you prefer not to use opposite colors on the color wheel, then don't. I have seen scrolls where the stripes were pinks and the gradations were purples. It works because the purples had no trace of pink and the pink stripes had no trace of purple.

You can use Rosie's Rainbow Flower project for examples of opposites on the color wheel. All the gradations are opposites of the main stripe colors within the same scroll shapes. Color wheels are a good resource and can usually be purchased at your local quilt store. There are also plenty of good books out there on color.

I believe most of us have excellent color sense unless we have color blindness. What I find most of my students want is assurance that they are making good color choices for their projects. Don't be afraid to try color combinations that seem scary. Sometimes the scary color is just what you need. Now notice I didn't say anything about ugly colors. Don't waste your money on colors you dislike. You won't like working with that fabric and when you look at your finished project, that ugly stuff will just take your attention away from the rest

3-D Explosion

of the design. So blow it off, pick another color, and move on!

It's time to figure out how much fabric you will need. The first step is to figure out how many templates you have that are labeled solid. That is how many steps in your gradation you will need. The illustrations we have been working with so far are the same as the large scroll in the Simple Sammy Scroll project. This scroll has 2 solids on one side and 3 solids on the other side. So we need 5 steps of gradation for a total of 5 fabrics.

I would recommend measuring the largest "solid" template, double that and then get that same amount of fabric for each of your gradations. Don't worry about grain line. Yes, you will have leftover fabric. When the fabrics go up on the design wall, you may want to change your mind about where a color goes. Now you have the choice to re-cut and enough fabric to do it. This is art, not science, and sometimes things just have to be changed.

As for the stripes, you could also measure your pieces keeping in mind the direction of the stripe. You could actually take your templates to the store and lay them out so you buy enough. Be sure to purchase an extra yard or two to give yourself the option to re-cut. Sometimes you need to change the direction of a stripe. Give yourself room to make choices. If you decide to do this, make sure to put your sewing order numbers on your master drawing too. That way you will be able to figure out where the templates go back into the design when it is on the design wall.

If you are using hand dyes or you are unsure about the colorfastness of your fabrics, pre-wash them. One of the steps in the process of making these quilts involves water and colors can run.

That is how you get started with your own design. To show you how to construct a scroll, I am going to use the first project, the Simple Sammy Scroll to go through the steps. I have provided template diagrams for each of the projects so that you can enlarge them to size using the enlarging techniques I described in the Blow Your Design Up chapter. These are all located at the back of the book, right before the Gallery. Each of these template diagrams have all the markings we have just discussed. There is also a marking called "glue." It is discussed in the next chapter along with the sewing. You will understand it better that way. So if designing your own scroll is just not your cup of tea, let's move on to the first project! And if it is for you, read through the Simple Sammy Scroll before you sew, so you can understand how to sew your project together.

Projects : See photographs for all the projects in the Gallery section

This part of the book has seven different projects. There is a template sheet provided for each project along with instructions on how large to blow it up at the end of the book on pages 74-80. There is also a pattern layout diagram to show how many of the template patterns are needed and in what direction they face. Some scroll designs are repeated and/or mirrored. Fabric requirements are very generous. You will have leftover fabric because these are art quilts and not simply squares that are easy to measure.

Please read through the first part of the book before you attempt any of the projects so that you can develop an understanding of how these projects are designed. Then read through the Simple Sammy Scroll project in order to understand the construction method. Once you have that knowledge, choosing your fabrics for your project will be much easier.

3-D Explosion

Simple Sammy Scroll : Glue, Masking Tape, a Light Box and Invisible thread are the tools of this trade!
(Getting your drawing off of the design wall and into fabric with the first project)
54" L X 41" W

Fabric supplies:
2½ yards of a lengthwise Bright Rainbow Stripe for "A" scroll
½ yard each of 2 purple gradations for "A" scroll
½ yard each of 3 blue gradations for "A" scroll

1½ yards of a lengthwise Black/Rainbow Stripe "B" scroll
½ yard each of 2 green gradations for "B" scroll

1 5/8 yd Background fabric

You have already learned how to draw your own design, make it the size you want and mark your templates for sewing. In order to illustrate the next steps of cutting apart your templates, attaching them to fabric and sewing your design together, I have designed the Simple Sammy Scroll. Most of the projects in this book are similar to this design.

This design has one complete scroll and another half scroll as part of the design. Take a look at the template page and you will notice that each scroll has a set of numbers and a letter designation as well. There are letters next to the numbers such as 1A, 2A, 3A,1B, 2B and 3B. Just as important are the letters that are written outside of the templates right above the corresponding scroll. I find this very useful, especially with complicated designs. You will be using your backgrounds as a guide, so you won't be throwing them out until the design is sewn together.

The first part of your mission is to enlarge this design. I enlarged mine 400% at a copy store. Notice how I have already reversed the design for you. After you blow up the design, you will layer your freezer paper on top of the enlarged design and trace it with a PENCIL onto freezer paper. Resist the urge to use a Sharpie, as it will probably damage your fabric in the last part of the process. Make sure to transfer all the markings.

There is a marking we haven't talked about yet. It is called "glue". This marking indicates which edges we are going to glue under in order to appliqué them on top of other edges. I find this is best explained as we are getting ready to sew our project together. If you are creating your own design, please read through the sewing instructions for a better understanding of which edges receive this sticky treatment and why. Then you will be able to add the glue marking to your design in the proper manner.

Let's start by cutting the templates apart. The first thing you need to do is to cut away the background of your freezer paper. <u>It's very important that you do this in one piece.</u> You will be putting this background piece back onto your design board so the "outline" can help you place your other templates back up on the board. Think of it as insurance. Cut in from one edge, then cut all the way around your design until the background separates into one piece. Put this background up on your design wall with the SHINY SIDE facing OUT.

Next cut the "B" scroll apart from the "A" scroll. Put it on the design wall in its empty space SHINY Side OUT, using the outline of the background to place it correctly.

Then continue on that "slide" outline and cut off the small part of the scroll that includes pieces 1A through 5A. Keep it in one piece for now and put it up on the design wall in its empty space, SHINY Side OUT. The piece of scroll left over should fit perfectly into the empty space left on the design wall SHINY side OUT. If it doesn't, something is placed in the wrong area and this is the best time to get it right.

It's time to cut smaller templates apart. Take the last template set with pieces 6A through 9A off the wall. First cut apart the curved spiral line. Then cut the straight lines and the templates will all come apart. Now put them all back up on the wall back in their original positions. Take the other half of the scroll off the wall with the group 1A to 5A. Cut apart the spiral. Then cut the templates apart along the straight lines. Put them back

3-D Explosion

on the wall in their original positions.

Now pull the "B" spiral off of the wall. Cut apart the spiral. Then cut apart the straight lines and separate the templates. Put them back on the wall.

Time for fabric! Heat up your iron. Press your fabrics so they are nice and smooth. Let's start with the Bright Rainbow stripe for the "A" scroll. Lay the fabric out on your ironing board with the WRONG side of the fabric up. Now grab your 8A template from your design wall. Always cut your largest template first! Lay it on top of the wrong side of the fabric with the SHINY Side DOWN. Line up your stripe guide lines (remember the group of three lines) with the stripes. This is your show piece, so look at where the colors in your stripe fall inside the template shape. Your design will be more pleasing to you if you have your favorite part of the stripe showing up in the biggest part of your show piece. When you have your template placed where you want, press the shiny side of the freezer paper template down onto the wrong side of your fabric and it will stick! You see, meat doesn't get to have all the fun after all!

Now it's time to cut the fabric. Leave ¼" of fabric beyond the freezer paper all the way around the template for seam allowance. Just eyeball it. Too big is better than too small. As my friend Ann says, "Chop the Chicken!" which means let's move onto another piece. Put your template covered fabric up on the design wall and grab your 6A template which is the small comma shape. With the shiny side down, lay the template onto the wrong side of the fabric and line up the stripe marks with your stripes in your fabric. When you are happy with your placement, press it on so that it sticks. Cut the template shape out, leaving ¼" of fabric sticking out all the way around as your seam allowance. Put it back on the design wall. Repeat these steps with 5A and then 3A. Please do only one template at a time. You don't want to lose one.

Next we grab our gradations. For the "A" scroll we have 2 purples and 3 blues. 7A is light purple and 9A is dark purple. 4A is dark blue, 2A is medium blue, and 1A is light blue. You will pull the templates off the wall one at a time and iron them onto the wrong side of their assigned fabric. Cut each template shape out of the fabric, leaving a ¼" seam allowance around each one. Put them back up on the wall as you go along.

On to the "B" scroll. You will need your black/rainbow fabric. 4B is your largest template, so place and cut that one out just as you did with the other striped templates so far. Repeat this with templates 5B and 2B.

Time for your green fabrics. Your 1B template will be cut out of the light green and your 3B template will be cut out of your dark green. Once they are all back up on the wall, it's time to evaluate your design.

Now you can see how your scroll is going to look. This is the point where you may choose to change something. Remember when I told you the fabric supply list is very generous? If you are completely satisfied with your design, then you have leftovers. If you have to re-cut something, then you have insurance, which you probably wouldn't notice unless you didn't have enough fabric to re-cut. Sometimes you may decide to change out a stripe or a gradation group entirely. This is another bonus of freezer paper. You can peel it off and press it onto more fabric quite a few times before it stops sticking.

Ready for the next step? It's almost time to sew. We will be joining these pieces together with machine appliqué using invisible thread. That means that we will fold some edges under, lay them on top of other edges, and zig zag over the top to hold the pieces together. Intrigued? Good.

Time to get out your trusty glue stick! Notice the shape of three dots on your template shapes that make up a triangular type of shape:

I have included this 3-Dot Triangle indicator on your templates throughout the projects in this book to show which edges to glue under. But first let me go over the rules so that you will understand how to do this on your own designs:

- We only glue straight edges at this stage.
- We only glue straight edges of cup, cone or half moon shapes.
- We don't glue straight edges of outside design line edges. If you do, it's not a horrid problem and you won't have to unglue it. The outside edges of your appliqué will be easier to deal with later and they will look better if you resist gluing them under right now.
- We will sew straight seams within each half of a scroll before we sew the spiral seam. More on this later.

I am going to show you shape by shape which edges are glued down and tell you why. Let's start with the 7A template with fabric on it. It's a cup shape. Look at the empty space you left on the design wall and see that neither one of the straight edges is an outside edge. Turn the template so that the rough paper side is facing up. Take your glue stick and run it along the one of the straight edges of the paper on your template shape. Note the 3-Dot Triangle shape on your template is your glue marker. Use your thumb and fold the seam allowance of the fabric along the straight edge of the template and onto the glue so it sticks to the back of the paper template. Now do the same to the other straight edge. Do not glue any curved edges. Put the template back up on the design wall.

Next get your 9A cone shape. See how one straight side is actually an outside design line edge? Resist gluing that edge. Instead, glue the other inside edge. You have the 3-Dot Triangle on your template just in case, but if this is your own design, then keep track of which edge you need to glue as you grab it off of the design wall.

Glue template 1A along its straight edge. Glue template 3A along both straight edges. Glue template 5A along the one straight edge that falls inside the design.

Glue template 2B along both straight edges. Glue template 4B along the inside straight edge. 5B has one straight edge, but it's an outside design line edge, so leave it until later. Let your glue dry.

I have made a mini step-by-step version of the Simple Sammy Scroll project. Follow along and I will show you how to sew these scrolls together! Here is a photo of all the pieces of the "A" scroll in the Simple Sammy Scroll project:

Step 1: Time to get the sewing machine ready. I wind my bobbin with invisible thread. Wind it slowly and fill it to about ¾ full. Put your bobbin in and thread up the top of your machine with the same invisible thread. I recommend an open-toe foot so that you can see where your needle is going down into the fabric. Set your machine to a zig zag stitch. Put a piece of paper underneath your machine foot and take enough stitches so that you can see them come out of the back side of the foot. They will probably be too wide and too long. Decrease your length and width of your stitch until it's about the same as the diagram below:

On my Bernina sewing machine the settings are stitch length = 1 and stitch width = 1. You may find that your machine performs better if you loosen your top tension a little. Once that is adjusted, it's time to sew. Pull out your light box and turn it on. Grab a roll of masking tape. Off we go!

Step 2: Start with templates 1A and 2A. Place 2A with the fabric right side up on the light box. You should be able to see the paper template outline through it. Look for the straight edge that lines up with 1A. Now take 1A and place the folded edge on top of 2A, lining up the folded edge with the template edge of 2A that you can see through the light box. Once that is lined up, look at the bottom of the template edges that you can see through the fabric and make sure that curved edge lines up. Your templates will sew back together to make the same shape you originally cut apart.

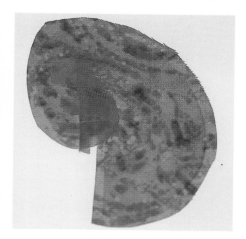

33

3-D Explosion

Put a piece of masking tape in the middle to hold both pieces together. Now look for the mark at the top that extends the half moon shape. You will see it inside the 2A shape. This is the top of the seam. Put a piece of masking tape with the bottom of the tape lining up right at the edge of that line across both pieces of fabric to indicate where to start sewing the seam.

Now take your templates to the sewing machine. You will begin your seam at the edge of the masking tape. You want your needle to enter the fabric on the side of the seam that has one layer of fabric right next to the fold. Then you want the needle to swing over the fold to enter the fabric though all three layers of fabric. Then swing back to the single layer of fabric right next to the fold. Continue all the way to the edges of the fabric, removing the tape as you go. Do not sew through the tape. Cut your threads.

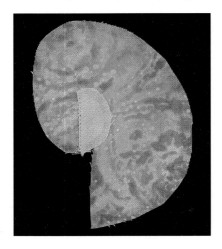

Step 3: Get 3A and the pieces you just stitched together and go back to the light box. Fold your 1A out of the way to expose the raw straight edge of 2A. Now lay 3A right on top of 2A matching up the template edges as you did before. Check the bottom of the template edges to see that they line up too. It looks like this:

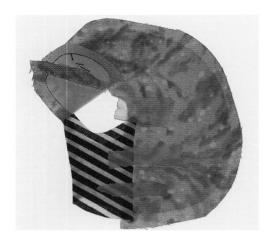

Now look for the registration mark that indicates where the seam starts. Place a piece of masking tape so that the bottom edge of the tape rests on that line. It indicates the beginning of the seam. Put more tape on to hold the rest of the seam together. Back to the sewing machine. Begin sewing right at the edge of the masking tape at the top of the seam and continue all the way off the edges of your fabric, removing the tape as you go. Cut your threads.

Step 4: Get your 4A piece and back to the light box. Fold your 2A out of the way to expose the straight edge that will sew to 4A. Lay 4A down on the light box first and then put the folded edge of 3A on top, lining up the straight edges as before. Check the bottom edge and make sure the templates line up there too. Sew the

3-D Explosion

seam as you did the others. Here is what your scroll looks like at this point:

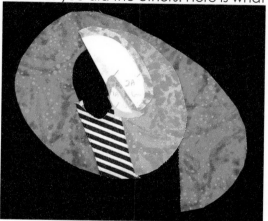

Step 5: Get 5A and attach it to 4A. Your scroll now looks like this:

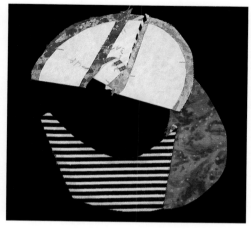

You have created a big snail! Set it aside and let's sew the other side of the scroll together.

Step 6: Take 6A and 7A to the light box. 7A lays on top of 6A, again lining up the straight edges of the templates and the bottom edge as well. Place a piece of tape in the middle of the seam to hold the pieces together. Look for the registration mark the point of the 6A and put a piece of masking tape there, lining up the registration mark with the bottom of the tape. This indicates the beginning of your seam. Now sew this seam just as you did the others.

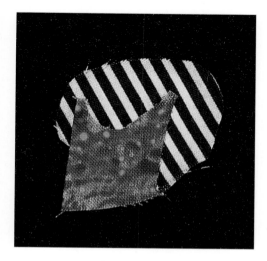

3-D Explosion

Step 7: Next we need the big slide template 8A. Fold 6A out of the way to reveal the side of 7A that will lay on top of 8A. Go to the light box and line them up, tape them up taking care to put your tape at the beginning of the seam and then sew them up.

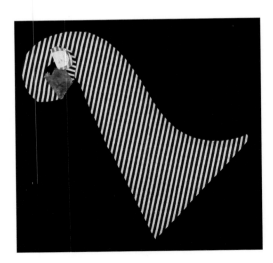

Step 8: Time for the 9A piece. It lays on top of the 8A piece. This is a long seam and has a couple of registration marks to line up along the seam line. Line it up, tape it up, and sew the seam all the way off the edge.

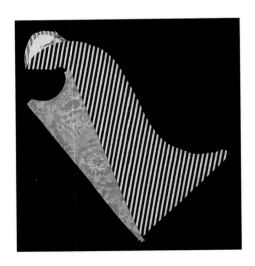

3-D Explosion

Step 9: Remember how you cut the curvy spiral lines of these scrolls apart before the straight lines? Now we will put the spiral seam back together. First we need to clip one side of the curved line. Starting at the inside concave curve of the 5A template, clip the seam allowance almost to the edge of the paper. Continue around the curve until you reach the point where 1A and 2A meet. Stop. Get the other half of the spiral and clip the same concave curve, stopping where 6A and 7A meet.

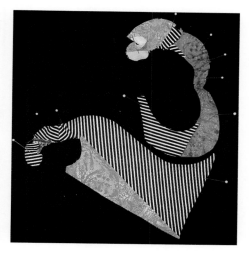

Step 10: Pick up one of the spirals and run glue along the same edge of the paper as the seam allowance that you just clipped. Fold the seam allowance of the fabric over and onto the back of the template. Work your way around the curve until it's done. Repeat with the other spiral. You will need to tuck the point of template 1A under. That folded edge will now lay on top of the raw edge of the same curve and cover it. Here is a photo of the seams glued:

Step 11: Back to the light box. Remember how we extended the seam lines down into the next template as a guide line? You should be able to see them through the light box. If your templates shifted a little bit, it's better to have the shape lay flat than to line up exactly. If you find your design is way off, check and see that the templates are sewn back together correctly.

3-D Explosion

Line up your spiral seam line and tape it down all the way around the spiral shape. At the beginning of the spiral there is a registration mark to indicate the beginning of the seam. Place the lower edge of a piece of masking tape along that line so that you know where to start your seam. More tape is better. Your shape is getting heavy now and it can pull apart on the way to the machine if you don't have enough tape. This is also where your extension table really comes in handy to support your templates.

Step 12: Begin sewing your spiral seam at the outside of the shape, starting your seam at the edge of the masking tape you used to indicate the beginning of the seam. Continue to sew the seam, pulling off the tape as you go until you reach the end of the spiral. Do a back-tack at the end to lock the thread. Now put it up on the design wall and admire your work!

Step 13: Next we are going to glue the outisde edges of the 6A-9A piece, but not all of them. Leave the long straight edge of 8A open. Now get your 1A-5A template piece. Begin by glueing the outside straight edge of 5A under. Continue over the top of 4A, stopping just before the registration mark. Leave the bottom open, as this part of the template will be covered by the 6A-9A piece. See the photograph below.

Step 14: The raw edge of 5A fits under the turned curved edge of 8A. Line them up on the light box fitting the template edges together. Look for the marking that lines up with the outside of 4A.

Sew this seam. Now glue down the last outside edge along 8A. We saved it for last so that our corners would fold under nicely. Step back and have a look at your creation on the design wall. Hubba hubba!

Step 15: Onto the "B" scroll. Line up 1B and 2B just like you did before. Tape and sew the seam. Get 3B and attach it. Now add 4B. Notice how 5B has a curved edge, but no straight edge that meets up with the rest of the group? Since it doesn't have a straight seam in common with the other templates, it will attach separately after the spiral seam is sewn.

Step 16: Clip the concave curved seam allowance starting on the 4B template all the way to the point of 1B. Glue, tape and sew as before. Now glue the outside edge of this shape, starting with the straight edge along 4B, over the top of 3B and stopping just short of the registration mark.

Step 17: Get the 5B template and glue the curved edge that will lay on top of 4B.

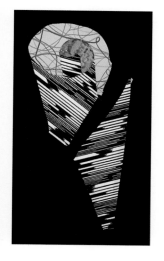

Step 18: Lay it on top of 4B, lining up the template edges. You also have the seam line extended down from the seam between 3B and 4B to help you line it up. Tape and sew together.

Step 19: Glue the rest of the outside of 3B and the straight edge of 5B under. Leave the bottom of 5B/4B open. Slip that raw edge under the "A" scroll, matching up the marks on the templates on the light box. Tape and sew. Your appliqué is done!!! Now let it dry completely. You don't want to appliqué soggy edges to your background.

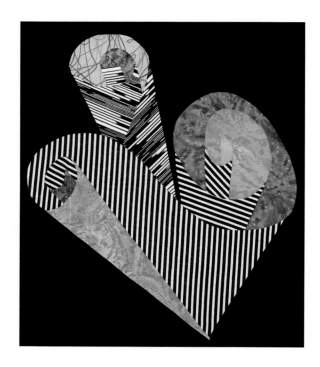

3-D Explosion

Time for background fabric. I think it's best to audition your scrolls on different backgrounds before committing to one. For the Simple Sammy Scroll I used a white background. All of the other projects are on black backgrounds because I believe black shows off the design best. But I have to admit the white background makes this scroll really look good! Try for fabrics that are more tone-on-tone or mottled looking. You want your audience to focus on your scroll.

I chose a 1 5/8 yard piece of fabric. Leave the selvages on and lay the fabric out on your design table right side up. (I use insulation boards that are 4' X 8'. I have them duct taped together like a hinge. When I open them up, I have an 8' X 8' surface that I can pin into.) Secure the corners of your background with pins or tape, depending on the surface that you are working on. Place your Simple Sammy Scroll appliqué on the background. Look at the photograph in the book for placement. When you are happy with your placement, grab your pins. Pin from the center out through the appliqué and the background fabric. This helps to stabilize the background. Now pin into the appliqué and through the background, parallel to the edges of the appliqué and very close together. Make sure your background stays as smooth as possible.

When you are done, undo your quilt top from the design board. Take the whole thing to your sewing machine. With the machine set up just as before with the invisible thread and the small zig zag, stitch all the way around the edges of your appliqué, removing the pins as you go. Take your time. Lock stitch the end to secure the thread.

After that it's time to take out the paper. First we are going to cut away the background fabric from underneath the appliqué shape. Clip into the background to make a hole underneath the appliqué. Now cut away the background to reveal the paper underneath, leaving a ¼" seam allowance inside the zig zag seam line you just sewed to attach the appliqué to your background.

Back to your design surface. Lay down enough dry towels to fit under the appliqué shape. Lay your quilt top on the dry towels, paper side up. Take more towels and get them nice and wet, almost dripping. Lay them on top of the paper area and let it soak for about 20 minutes. Now it should be time to pull the paper out and it should come easily. If not, let it soak a little longer and try again. Remove all the paper and let your top dry. You could iron it dry, but be careful not to scorch or stretch your fabric.

You are done with your top! For the final step in making a simply fabulous art quilt, turn to the chapter on Quilting.

3-D Explosion

Spinning Star Scrolls
© 2004 by Cara Gulati

Pattern design layout

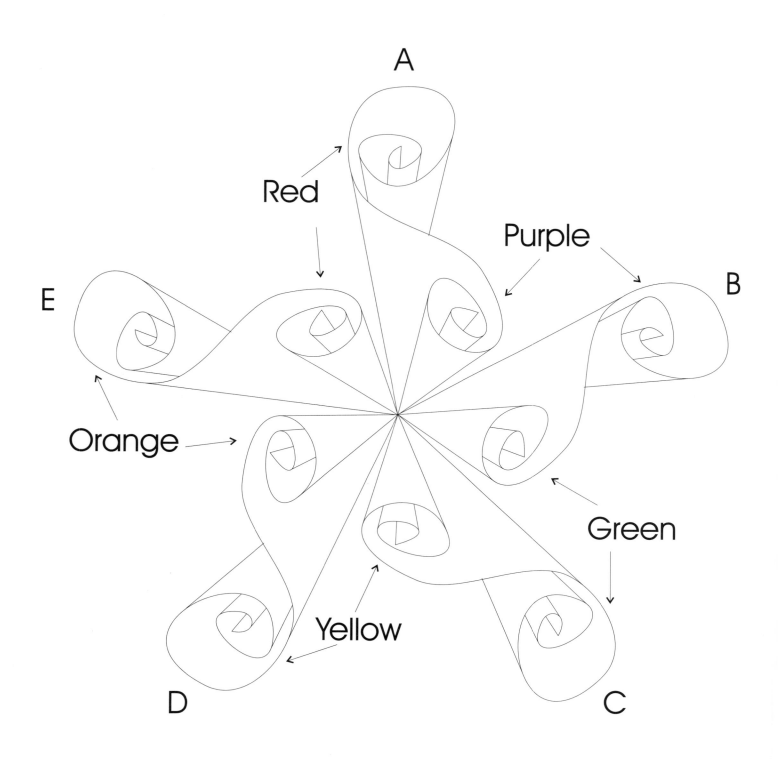

A

Red

Purple

B

E

Orange

Green

Yellow

D

C

Spinning Star Scrolls
66" Square

This is a very unique quilt design. It is composed of 5 scrolls, all the same. I have used the same stripe for all 5 scrolls. I varied the gradations and used them in the order of the color wheel to bring the eye around the star.

Generous Fabric Requirements:
4 yards of a lengthwise Blue Stripe: I find a skinny stripe works best with this skinny scroll.

½ yards of each of the following:
Light, Medium, and Dark Green
Light, Medium, and Dark Yellow
Light, Medium, and Dark Orange
Light, Medium, and Dark Red
Light, Medium, and Dark Purple

Background:
About 4 yards of black.

Template Instructions:
Enlarge your Spinning Star Scroll template pattern 285%. Notice how I have "WRONG SIDE" on the template pattern. It has been reversed for you to save time. You will need to trace a total of 5 freezer paper template sets of this scroll design. Label the first set with A's just like the enlargement. Change the A's to B's for the second set, and repeat changing the third set to C's, the fourth set to D's and the fifth set to E's. Put them up in alphabetical order on your design wall, just like the photograph and pattern layout, with the shiny side of the paper facing out.

Cutting Instructions:

Step 1: Cut all the templates apart and put them back up on the design wall. Remember to keep your background freezer paper shape of each of your templates. It helps to have the outline of the design when placing the templates back up on the design wall.

Step 2: Starting with your stripe, iron all the large #9 template pieces to the wrong side of the fabric, making sure to follow the stripe guides. Cut them out leaving a ¼" seam allowance of fabric all the way around the outside of the template shape. Put them all back up on the wall in their respective scrolls. Repeat with all the stripe templates 3, 5, 6, and 7 in all the scrolls working from the largest shape to the smallest.

Step 3: Get your gradations and look at the photograph of the Spinning Star Scrolls in the gallery section. Notice how the bottom part of one scroll has light and medium purple fabrics in the cup and cone section. If you look at the next scroll to the right, the top has light, medium, and dark purples in the horseshoe and comma pieces at the top. Notice that on the bottom part of that same purple-topped scroll there are light and medium greens in the bottom cup and cone section. Then look to the next scroll to the right of that one and there are light, medium, and dark greens in the top horseshoe shapes of that scroll. You can see this color pattern repeating all the way around the star. The color order is Purple, Green, Yellow, Orange, and Red. Keeping that in mind, work with one gradation group at a time. Take the templates off your design wall one at a time. It will help to refer to the photograph as you go along. Cut out the following template shapes for each scroll, cutting the fabric ¼" larger than the template for seam allowance:

Cut a #4 and a #8 from each light color.
Cut a #2 and a #10 for each medium color.
Cut a #1 for each dark color.

Sewing Instructions:
These instructions are specific to this pattern. General sewing instructions are included in the Simple Sammy Scroll project chapter.

Step 1: Glue the seam allowance under on the marked straight edges of 1A, 3A, 5A, 6A, 8A and 10A. Sew pieces 1A - 5A into a scroll unit. Sew pieces 6A – 10A into a scroll unit. Repeat for scrolls B, C, D, and E.

Step 2: Glue the outside seam allowance under around the 1-5 units from the straight edge of 5, up and over 4 and stopping just before the registration mark.
Glue the outside seam allowance under around the 6-10 units along the straight edge of 10, up and over 9 all the way to the point. (See diagram.)

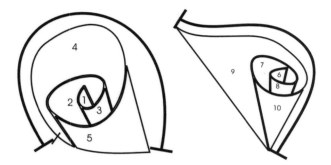

Step 3: Slip the 1-5 unit under the glued edge of the 6-10 unit, lining up with the marks on the slide template and sew them together. Last, glue down the last straight edge of the #9. Repeat this for all the scrolls.

Step 4: Get your background ready. Piece it to make a 70" square. I have allowed 4" in each direction for quilting shrinkage. Fold it in half in both directions and find the center. Lay down all five scrolls, minding the color order, with all the points meeting in the center of the background. Move them until they look even. Then walk around to another side of the quilt top and adjust them. Keep walking around and adjusting your scrolls until they look evenly spaced all the way around. Take a short break to walk away. Maybe have chocolate! Go back and look one more time. Pin them to your background. Appliqué your scrolls down, cut way the back and take out the paper. Time to quilt and bind!

3-D Explosion

3-D Explosion

Beautiful Butterfly
© 2004 by Cara Gulati
Pattern Layout Diagram

3-D Explosion

Beautiful Butterfly
74" W X 41"L

This fun quilt provides us with a marvelously mirrored image!

Generous Fabric Requirements:
4 yards of a lengthwise colorful stripe

½ yard of each of the following:
Light, Medium, and Dark Red/Purple
Medium and Dark Blue/Purple

¼ yard for the Butterfly body-I used a black print. Try something more noticeable!

Background:
2¼ yards of 44" wide fabric

Template Instructions:
Enlarge your Beautiful Butterfly template pattern 380%. Notice how I have "WRONG SIDE" on the template pattern. Once you have your enlargement, turn it over and trace the design and all the markings with a Sharpie. Instead of WRONG SIDE, write RIGHT SIDE. You will need to trace a total of 2 freezer paper template sets of this scroll design in pencil, one from the WRONG SIDE and one from the RIGHT SIDE. Label the first set with A's just like the enlargement. Change all the A's to B's for the second set. Put them up on your design wall, just like the photograph and pattern layout, with the shiny side of the paper facing out. You will only need one body.

Cutting Instructions:
Step 1: Cut all the templates apart and put them back up on the design wall. Remember to keep the freezer paper backgrounds of each of your templates. It helps to have the outline of the design when placing the templates back up on the design wall.

Step 2: Starting with your stripe, iron on the large 10A and 10B template pieces to the wrong side of the fabric, making sure to follow the stripe guides. Cut them out leaving a ¼" seam allowance of fabric all the way around the outside of the template shape. Put them back up on the wall. Repeat with all the stripe templates for A and B working from the largest shape to the smallest in this order: 8, 4, 6, 5 and then 2. Do them one a time.

Step 3: Get your gradations. Pull the templates off your design wall one at a time. Cut out the following template shapes, cutting the fabric ¼" larger than the template for seam allowance:
Cut 11 A and B from the light Red/Purple
Cut 9 A and B from the medium Red/Purple
Cut 7 A and B from the dark Red/Purple
Cut 1 A and B from the dark Blue/Purple
Cut 3 A and B from the medium Blue/Purple

Step 4: The body templates 12, 13 and 14 are all cut from the same fabric. Have fun with this one!

Sewing Instructions:
These instructions are specific to this pattern. General sewing instructions are included in the Simple Sammy Scroll project chapter.

Step 1: Glue the seam allowance under along the marked straight edges of 2A, 4A, 5A, 7A, 9A and 11A. Sew pieces 1A through 4A into a scroll unit. Sew pieces 5A though 11A into a scroll unit. Repeat for the B scroll.

Step 2: Glue the outside seam allowance under around the 1-4 A and B units from the straight edge of 4, up and over 3 and stopping just before the registration mark. Glue the outside seam allowance under around the 5-11 units along the straight edge of 11, up and over 10 all the way to the point. (See diagram.)

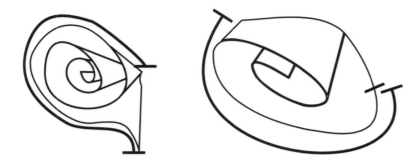

Step 3: Now slip the 1-4 unit under the glued edge of the 5-11 unit, lining up with the marks on the slide template and sew them together. Glue down the last straight edge of the #10.

Step 4: Time for the body. Glue the seam allowance edges of all three body pieces under. Matching the marks, just barely overlap the round head (12) on top of the middle body (13) and sew a few stitches. Now overlap the middle body on top of the bottom body (14) and sew a few stitches to hold it together. Now lay the whole body on top of one of the wings, matching the markings, and sew it together. Repeat with the other wing.

Step 5: Get your background ready. I have allowed 3" in each direction for quilting shrinkage. Fold in half in both directions and find the center. Place the body in the middle and center the butterfly wings so that they fall in the middle with the same amount of background above and below them. Move them until they look even. Then walk around to another side of the quilt top and adjust them. Keep walking around and adjusting your Beautiful Butterfly until it looks evenly spaced all the way around. Take a short break to walk away. Maybe have a soda. Go back and look one more time. Pin it to your background. Appliqué your butterfly down, cut away the back and take out the paper. Time to quilt and bind!

3-D Explosion

Reflections
© 2004 by Cara Gulati
Pattern layout diagram

3-D Explosion

Reflections
41" Square

Here is a smaller design. I have taken a simple scroll shape and added a half scroll to it. Then I mirrored the scroll. After that I mirrored both of those designs. They all have the same perspective point in the center. The result looks like a reflection. Notice how the dots in the orange fabric look stripy, which works as a stripe in this design.

Generous Fabric Requirements:
2 yards of a lengthwise Blue Batik stripe
1 yard of an Orange Dotted "stripe"

½ yards if the following:
Light and Dark Yellow/Green
Light and Dark Orange
Light Fuchsia and Dark Purple

Background:
1¼ yard of 44" wide fabric

Template Instructions:
Enlarge your Reflections template pattern 200%. Notice how I have "WRONG SIDE" on the template pattern. Once you have your enlargement, turn it over and trace the design and all the markings with a Sharpie onto the other side. Instead of WRONG SIDE, write RIGHT SIDE on your sharpie tracing.

You will need to trace a total of 4 freezer paper template sets of this scroll design, 2 from the WRONG SIDE and 2 from the RIGHT SIDE. Label the first set with A's and B's just like the enlargement. Change the A/B designations to G/H for the second WRONG SIDE set. Change the A/B to C/D for the first set traced from the RIGHT SIDE and then to E/F for the second set traced from the RIGHT SIDE. Put them up on your design wall, just like the photograph and pattern layout, with the shiny side of the paper facing out.

Cutting Instructions:
Step 1: Cut all the templates apart and put them back up on the design wall. Remember to keep your freezer paper backgrounds of each of your templates. It helps to have the outline of the design when placing the templates back up on the design wall.
Starting with your blue stripe, iron on all the large 8A, 8C, 8E and 8G template pieces to the wrong side of the fabric, making sure to follow the stripe guides. Cut them out leaving a ¼" seam allowance of fabric all the way around the outside of the template shape. Put them all back up on the wall in their respective scrolls. Repeat with all the blue stripe templates 2,4, 5 and 6 of scrolls A, C, E and G. Work from the largest shape to the smallest.

Step 2: Next get the orange stripe. When you look at the photograph, you will notice that the orange "stripe" is not consistent in its direction. I was running low on this fabric and it was perfect for this quilt. Substitutions just didn't make the grade. So I used it anyway and I think it looks great! It works because the blue stripe is the main event and each of the orange scrolls sits at a different angle.

Step 3: Iron on all the large 5B, 5D, 5F and 5H template pieces to the wrong side of the orange striped fabric, making sure to follow the stripe guides. Cut them out leaving a ¼" seam allowance of fabric all the way around the outside of the template shape. Put them all back up on the wall in their respective scrolls. Repeat with templates 4 and 2 of scrolls B, D, F and H to finish the stripes.

3-D Explosion

Step 4: Gradations. There are three gradation sets. Cut one each of the following one at a time and put them back up on the wall as you go:

Light Orange: 1A, 1C, 1E and 1G
Dark Orange: 3A, 3C, 3E and 3G
Light Green: 1B, 1D, 1F, and 1H
Dark Green: 3B, 3D, 3F, and 3 H
Fuchsia: 7A, 7C, 7 E and 7G
Purple: 9A, 9C, 9E and 9G

Sewing Instructions:
These instructions are specific to this pattern. General sewing instructions are included in the Simple Sammy Scroll project chapter.

Step 1: Glue the seam allowance under along the marked straight edges of 2A, 4A, 5A, 7A, 9A, 2B, and 4B. Sew pieces 1A through 4A into a scroll unit. Sew pieces 5A through 9A into a scroll unit. Sew 1B through 4B into a scroll unit. 5B attaches to the B scroll a little differently, so we'll get to that later. Repeat for the rest of the scrolls.

Step 2: Glue the outside seam allowance under around the 1-4 units of scrolls A, C, E and G from the straight edge of 4, up and over 3 and stopping just before the registration mark. Glue the outside seam allowance under around the 5-9 units of scrolls A, C, E and G along the straight edge of 9, up and over 8 all the way to the point.

Step 3: Glue the outside seam allowance under around the 1-4 units of scrolls B, D, F and H from the straight edge of 4, up and over 3 and stopping just before the registration mark. Glue the concave curve under along the top of 5B, 5D, 5F and 5H.

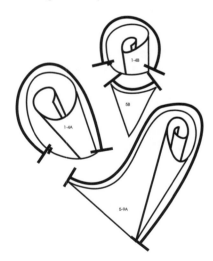

Step 4: Now slip the 1-4A unit under the glued edge of the 5-9 A unit, lining up with the marks on the slide template and sew them together. Repeat with C, E, and G units.
Lay the glued edge of the 5B template on top of the 1-4B unit, lining up the marks and sew them together. Glue the straight edge along the 5 template, but not the bottom. Repeat with scrolls D, F, and H.

3-D Explosion

Step 5: Slip the B template under the A template, lining up the marks, and sew it on. Repeat, attaching D to C, F to E and H to G.

Step 6: Glue the last straight edges of the 8 templates under.

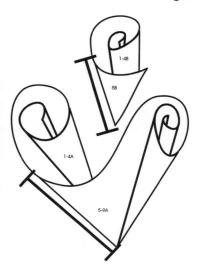

Step 7: Get your background ready. Use the whole square. I have allowed 3" in each direction for quilting shrinkage. Fold in half in both directions and find the center. Lay down all four scroll sets, minding the layout in the photograph, with all points meeting in the center of the background. Move them until they look even. Then walk around to another side of the quilt top and adjust them. Keep walking around and adjusting your scrolls until they look evenly spaced all the way around. Take a short break to walk away. Go back and look one more time. Pin them to your background. Appliqué your scrolls down, cut way the back and take out the paper. Time to quilt and bind!

3-D Explosion

Framed!
© 2004 by Cara Gulati
Pattern layout diagram

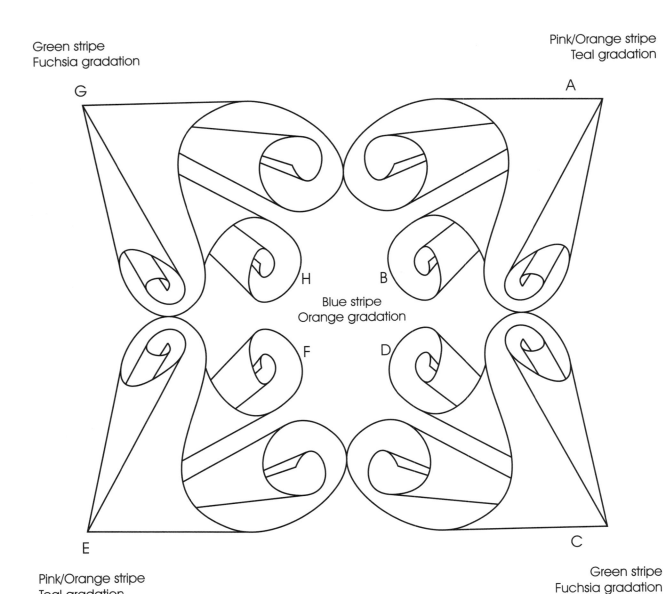

Green stripe
Fuchsia gradation

Pink/Orange stripe
Teal gradation

G

A

H

B

Blue stripe
Orange gradation

F

D

E

C

Pink/Orange stripe
Teal gradation

Green stripe
Fuchsia gradation

3-D Explosion

Framed!
40" W X 36"L

This quilt includes repetition, mirroring and four perspective points instead of one. When I designed this quilt I thought that it would be fun to use the scroll shapes like a picture frame. When they were done, I decided that the frame would be the quilt design! This design uses the same shape in the Reflections project, but the stripes face different ways.

Generous Fabric Requirements:
1½ yards of the following lengthwise stripes:
Green Stripe
Blue Stripe
Peach Stripe

½ yard each of the following:
Light and Dark Pink
Light and Dark Orange
Light and Dark Teal

Background fabric:
1¼ yard of 44" wide fabric

Template Instructions:
Enlarge your Framed! template pattern 210%. Notice how I have "WRONG SIDE" on the template pattern. Once you have your enlargement, turn it over and trace the design and all the markings with a Sharpie. Instead of WRONG SIDE, write RIGHT SIDE.
You will need to trace a total of 4 freezer paper template sets of this scroll design, 2 from the WRONG SIDE and 2 from the RIGHT SIDE. Label the first set with A's and B's just like the enlargement. Change the A/B designations to E/F for the second WRONG SIDE set. Change the A/B to C/D for the first set traced from the RIGHT SIDE and then to G/H for the second set traced from the RIGHT SIDE. Put them up on your design wall, just like the photograph and pattern layout, with the shiny side of the paper facing out.

Cutting Instructions:
Step 1: Cut all the templates apart and put them back up on the design wall. Remember to keep the freezer paper backgrounds of each of your templates. It helps to have the outline of the design when placing the templates back up on the design wall.

Step 2: Starting with your blue stripe, iron on all the large 5B, 5F, 5D and 5H template pieces to the wrong side of the fabric, making sure to follow the stripe guides. Cut them out leaving a ¼" seam allowance of fabric all the way around the outside of the template shape. Put them all back up on the wall in their respective scrolls. Repeat with all the blue striped templates 2, and 4 of scrolls B, F, D and H sets working from the largest shape to the smallest.

Step 3: Next get the pink/orange stripe. When you look at the photograph, you will notice that the pink/orange stripe appears on opposite sides of the design. Iron on the large 8A and 8E template pieces to the wrong side of the pink/orange striped fabric, making sure to follow the stripe guides. Cut them out leaving a ¼" seam allowance of fabric all the way around the outside of the template shape. Put them both back up on the wall in their respective scrolls. Repeat with templates 2, 4, 5 and 6 of scrolls A and E.

Step 4: Now get the green stripe. When you look at the photograph, you will notice that the green stripe also appears on opposite sides of the design. Iron on the large 8C and 8G template pieces to the wrong side of the green striped fabric, making sure to follow the stripe guides. Cut them out leaving a ¼" seam allowance of fabric all the way around the outside of the template shape. Put them both back up on the wall in their respective scrolls. Repeat with templates 2,4,5 and 6 of scrolls C and G.

3-D Explosion

Step 5: Gradations. There are two gradation sets. Cut each of the following one at a time and put them back up on the wall as you go:

Light Orange: 1B, 1D, 1F and 1H
Dark Orange: 3B, 3D, 3F and 3H
Light Fuchsia: 3C, 7C, 3G, and 7G
Dark Fuchsia: 1C, 9C, 1G and 9G
Light Teal: 3A, 7A, 3E and 7E
Dark Teal: 1A, 9A, 1E and 9E

Sewing Instructions:
These instructions are specific to this pattern. General sewing instructions are included in the Simple Sammy Scroll project chapter.

Step 1: Glue the seam allowance under along the marked straight edges of 2A, 4A, 5A, 7A, 9A, 2B, and 4B. Sew pieces 1A through 4A into a scroll unit. Sew pieces 5A through 9A into a scroll unit. Sew 1B through 4B into a scroll unit. 5B attaches to the B scroll a little differently but we'll get to that later. Repeat for the rest of the scrolls.

Step 2: Glue the outside seam allowance under around the 1-4 A, C, E and G units from the straight edge of 4, up and over 3 and stopping just before the registration mark.
Glue the outside seam allowance under around the 5-9 A, C, E and G units along the straight edge of 9, up and over 8 all the way to the point.

Step 3: Glue the outside seam allowance under around the 1-4 of the B, D, F and H units from the straight edge of 4, up and over 3 and stopping just before the registration mark. Glue the concave curve under along the top of 5B, 5D, 5F and 5H.

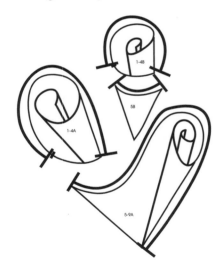

Step 4: Now slip the 1-4A unit under the glued edge of the 5-9 A unit, lining up with the marks on the slide template and sew them together. Repeat with C, E, and G units.
Lay the glued edge of the 5B template on top of the 1-4B unit, lining up the marks and sew them together. Glue the straight edge along the 5 template, but not the bottom. Repeat with scrolls D, F, and H.

Step 5: Slip the B template under the A template, lining up the marks, and sew it on. Repeat, attaching D to C, F to E and H to G.

Step 6: Glue the last straight edges of the 8 templates under.

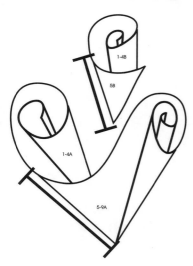

Step 7: Get your background ready. Cut your fabric down to a 40" length and leave the 44" width. I have allowed 4" in each direction for quilting shrinkage. Fold in half in both directions and press lightly with an iron so you can easily locate the center seams in both directions. Lay down all four scroll sets, minding the layout in the photograph, with all points pointing at the corners of the background and the scrolls facing the center. Notice how the edges of the scrolls touch in the photograph. Move them until they look even. Then walk around to another side of the quilt top and adjust them. Keep walking around and adjusting your scrolls until they look evenly spaced all the way around. Take a short break to walk away. Maybe have ice cream. Go back and look one more time. Pin them to your background. Appliqué your scrolls down, cut away the back and take out the paper. Time to quilt and bind!

3-D Explosion

Rosie's Rainbow Flower
© 2004 by Cara Gulati

Pattern layout

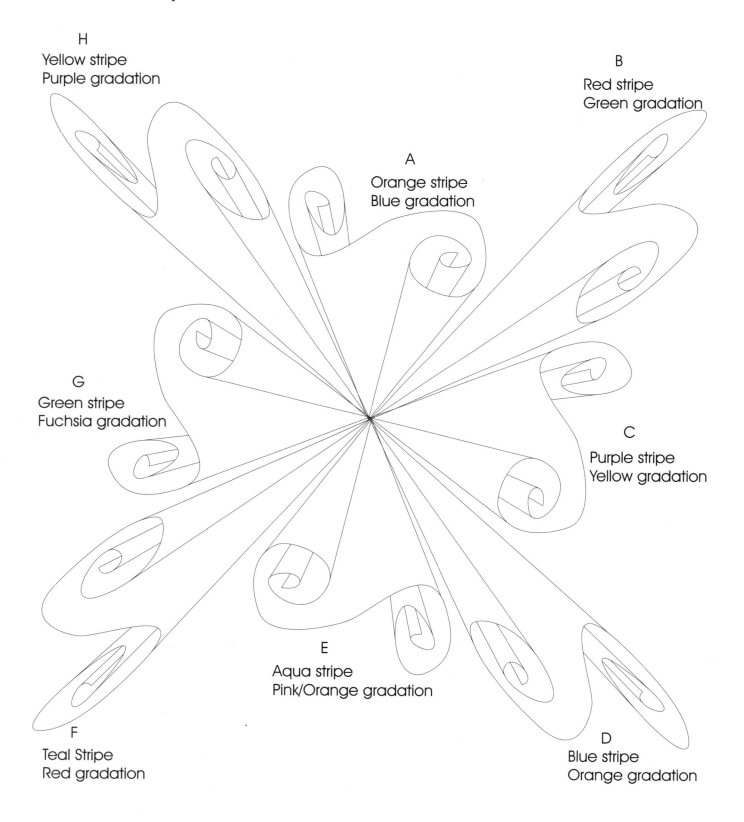

H
Yellow stripe
Purple gradation

B
Red stripe
Green gradation

A
Orange stripe
Blue gradation

G
Green stripe
Fuchsia gradation

C
Purple stripe
Yellow gradation

E
Aqua stripe
Pink/Orange gradation

F
Teal Stripe
Red gradation

D
Blue stripe
Orange gradation

Rosie's Rainbow Flower
80" Square

Computer drawing programs can make designing a blast. I had a simple scroll design that I stretched in different directions to play with it. I knew I wanted 8 scrolls to make a giant flower and I think it turned out pretty good! There are four long, skinny scrolls and four fat, squatty scrolls. They all face the same direction.

In the middle of the design there is a round shape that is appliquéd on top. All the points at the end of the scrolls will be cut away. I could design the scrolls without the points, but I think it's much easier to line the scrolls up on the background with their points before sewing them down.

Generous Fabric Requirements:
1½ yards of each of the following lengthwise stripes:
Yellow, Orange, Red, Purple, Blue, Aqua, Teal, and Yellow/Green

½ yard of each of the following gradations:
Light, light medium, medium dark, and dark Purple (goes with yellow stripe)
Light, light medium, medium dark, and dark Blue (goes with orange stripe)
Light, light medium, medium dark, and dark Teal (goes with red stripe)
Light, light medium, medium dark, and dark Yellow (goes with purple stripe)
Light, light medium, medium dark, and dark Orange (goes with blue stripe)
Light, light medium, medium dark, and dark Pinky/Orange (goes with aqua stripe)
Light, light medium, medium dark, and dark Red/Orange (goes with teal stripe)
Light, light medium, medium dark, and dark Fuchsia (goes with yellow/green stripe)

Background:
4¾ yards of 44" wide fabric.
I used a beautiful cotton sateen for the background of this quilt because it had such nice sheen. It was very difficult to work with in such a large size. I would recommend using something much more stable.

Template Instructions:
Enlarge your Rosie's Rainbow Flower template pattern 400%. Notice how I have "WRONG SIDE" on the template pattern. It has been reversed for you to save time. You will need to trace a total of 8 freezer paper template sets, 4 of each scroll design on the template page. Label the first set with A's just like the enlargement. Change the A's to C's for the second set, to E's for the third set and G's for the fourth set. Change the B's to D's for the second set, then F's for the third set, and then H's for the fourth set. Put them up in alphabetical order on your design wall, just like the photograph and pattern layout, with the shiny side of the paper facing out. You will only need one center circle template.

Cutting Instructions:
Step 1: Cut all the templates apart and put them back up on the design wall. Remember to keep your freezer paper backgrounds of each of your templates. It helps to have the outline of the design when placing the templates back up on the design wall. Cut out one yellow center circle and set it aside.

Each scroll has a different stripe and a different set of light-to-dark color gradations. The stripes and gradations in each scroll are opposite on the color wheel. The colors are designed to go around the design in the order of the color wheel with the stripe colors running clockwise and the gradation groups running counter clockwise.

Step 2: Pair up your stripes with their corresponding color gradation sets. Referring to the photograph and pattern sheet for placement, pin the fabric sets up on the design wall near the scroll from which they will be cut. That way you can make sure you like your color and placement selection before you actually cut them out.

3-D Explosion

Step 3: Cut out each scroll one at a time. Start with the stripe and cut out the largest template first, which is number 8. After pressing the template onto the wrong side of the fabric, remember to cut a ¼" seam allowance of fabric all the way around the outside of the template. Put it back up on the design wall. Then cut out templates 2, 4, 5 and 6, making sure you use the stripe directional markings and leave a ¼" seam allowance around the outside of those template shapes too. Cut out one scroll at a time, piece by piece, and put them right back up on the design wall. Cut out the stripe templates for all the scrolls.

Step 4: Now for the gradation sets. Start with one scroll. Any one will do. Using the color gradation set pinned onto your design wall for that scroll, cut out template number 3 in the light value, template number 1 in the medium dark value, template number 9 in the light medium value and template 7 in the dark value. Don't forget to leave the ¼" seam allowance all the way around the outside of the templates. Put them all back onto the design wall. Repeat with the rest of the scrolls.

Sewing Instructions
These instructions are specific to this pattern. General sewing instructions are included in the Simple Sammy Scroll project chapter.

Step 1: Glue the seam allowance under along the marked straight edges of 2, 4, 5, 7 and 9 for every scroll. . Sew pieces 1A through 4A into a scroll unit. Sew pieces 5A through 9A into a scroll unit. Repeat for the rest of the scrolls.

Step 2: Glue the seam allowance edges of the circle under. Set aside.

Step 3: Glue the outside seam allowance under around the 1-4 units from the straight edge of 4, up and over 3 and stopping just before the registration mark. Glue the outside seam allowance under around the 5-9 units along the straight edge of 9, up and over 8, all the way to the point. (See diagram.)

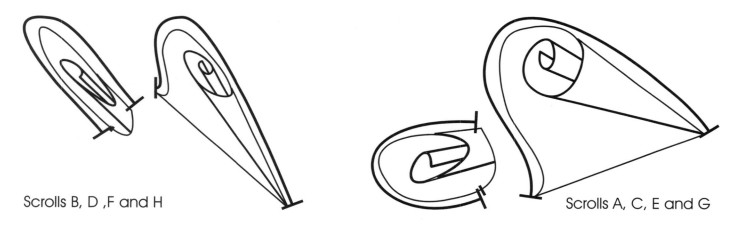

Scrolls B, D ,F and H   Scrolls A, C, E and G

Step 4: Now slip the 1-4 unit under the glued edge of the 5-9 unit, lining up with the marks on the slide template and sew them together. Last, glue down the last straight edge of the #8. Repeat this for all the scrolls.

Step 5: Get your background ready. Piece it to make an 84" square. I have allowed 4" in each direction for quilting shrinkage. Fold in half in both and find the center. Lay down all eight scrolls, minding the color order, all points meeting in the center of the background. Move them until they look even. Then walk around to another side of the quilt top and adjust them. Keep walking around and adjusting your scrolls until they look evenly spaced all the way around. Take a short break to walk away. Maybe make brownies. Go back and look one more time. Now add the center circle. Pin all the pieces to your background. Pin on the yellow center. Appliqué it all down, cut away the back and take out the paper. Time to quilt and bind!

3-D Explosion

Colossal Scrolls
© 2004 by Cara Gulati
Pattern Layout Diagram

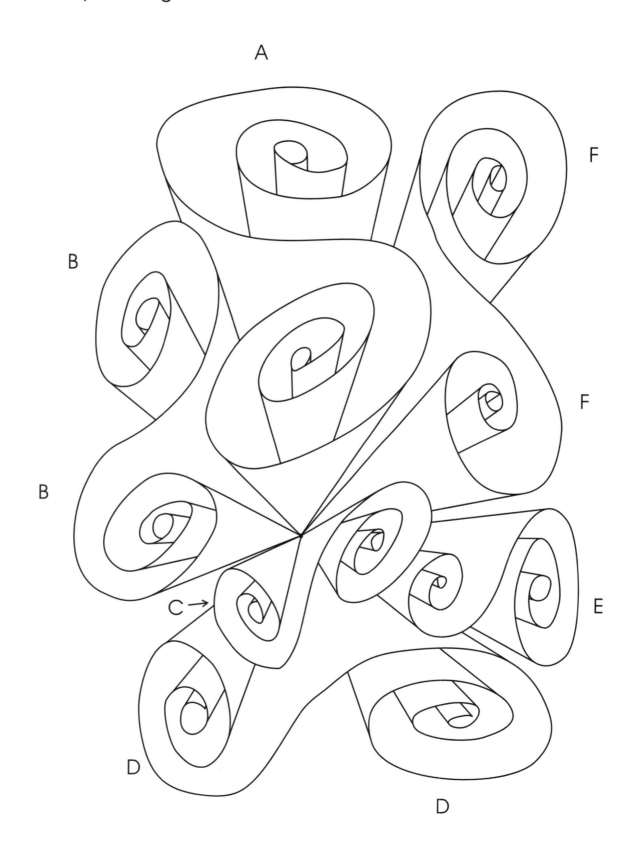

Colossal Scrolls
108" L X 87" W

This is the original quilt that started my journey into a series of 3-D quilts. It's quite large at 110" X 87". I designed this quilt with pencil and paper and used an overhead projector to enlarge the design. I knew when the bottom of the design hit the floor and the top of the design hit the ceiling, that it was just the right size.

I have been hauling this giant quilt around for awhile now. Its sheer size and complexity blows people away when they see it for the first time. And so, by popular demand, I have included it as a project in my book.

Since I made Colossal Scrolls, I have learned a few things about designing these quilts. I took the liberty of simplifying a few lines and adjusting some of the curves just a little bit so they look better.

A few words about enlarging this design. To make it the colossal size that my quilt is, I would recommend you use the overhead projector method and skip the trip to the copy shop. Enlarging the design with a copy machine may produce some really thick lines that may be hard to deal with. The design by itself measures about 88" X 63".

Fabrics:
This project is a true art quilt. Some of these pieces are quite large. Some have stripes that fit the formula I have given you and some do not. I am including a list of the colors and type of fabrics I used in the quilt as a guideline, but not amounts needed. This is not a quilt you will produce just like the photograph, but something you can lend your own style to. Most likely you will not want to make it quite as large as I did. I will leave it to you to decide which fabrics to use where. Use the photograph as a reference for the stripe direction. If I were to make this quilt today, I would have the stripe directions make more obvious changes.

Scroll "A"
Stripe: Red/Green batik
Yellow/Green hand dyed gradation
Blue/Green hand dyed gradation

Scroll "B"
Stripe: Green multicolored shibori hand dye
Red Ginkgo hand painted fabric

Scroll "C"
Stripe: Blue Circles hand painted fabric
Blue/Purple hand dye

Scroll "D"
Stripe: Blue/Green batik
Mustard and Yellow/Green hand dyes
Mustard, Orange and Red hand dyes

Scroll "E"
Stripe: Yellow/mustard hand painted
Red, Orange and gold hand painted

Scroll "F"
Stripe: Pink/Rainbow batik
Red/Purple hand-dye

Template Instructions:
Enlarge your Colossal Scrolls template pattern 1000% (about 88" X 63") with an overhead projector. Notice how I have "WRONG SIDE" on the template pattern. It has been reversed for you to save time. You will need to make one master pattern from the projected image and then one freezer paper template from the WRONG SIDE of the master pattern.

Cutting Instructions:
Cut all the templates apart and put them back up on the design wall. Remember to keep your freezer paper background of your templates. It helps to have the outline of the design when placing the templates back up on the design wall.

Sewing Tips:
There is a piece on this quilt that you haven't seen in the other quilts. In the center of some of the scrolls there is an organic round shape instead of a half moon or a comma shape. Sometimes it is split in half like on pieces 1F and 2F. Sew 2F on top of 1F. Construct the rest of scroll as explained in the Simple Sammy Scroll project. Then, after you sew the spiral seam, appliqué the organic round shape on top, lining it up with the corresponding marks.

Check out 14A. You will notice that it doesn't attach directly to the rest of the A scroll with a straight seam to make it part of a scroll. When this happens with a design, you sew it on after the other scroll shapes are done and ready to be joined together. So in this case, you make scroll 1A-6A and 7A –13A. Then join those two together. Then join 14A to that group.

Sewing Instructions:
This is an advanced project. These instructions are specific to this pattern. General sewing instructions are included in the Simple Sammy Scroll project chapter.

There are some pieces that are so small that the glue markings cannot be seen in the template pattern. Make sure to glue the straight edges of 2A, 8A, 2B, 9C, 2E, 8E, and 1F.

3-D Explosion

Here is a diagram to help you see the scrolls pulled apart from each other and pulled in half. It will help you to see the design along with the pattern sheet and the photograph.

3-D Explosion

Step 1: The "A" scroll. Sew the 1A-6A small half of the scroll. Sew the 7A-13A large half of the scroll. Glue the top curve seam of 14A, the outside of the A1-6 half scroll except the bottom, and the curve edge of A7-13 according to the diagram. Then put 14A on top of the big scroll, taking care to line it up with the registration marks, and sew them together. Lay the A7-13 scroll on top of the A 1-6 scroll matching the registration marks, and sew them together. Now finish gluing down all the outside edges.

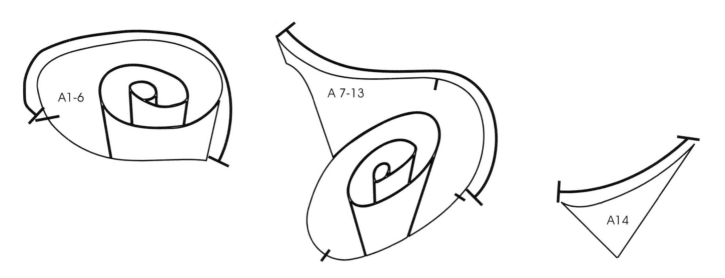

Step 2: The "B" Scroll. Sew the 1B-6B small half of the scroll. Sew the 7B-13B large half of the scroll. Glue the outside of the B1-6 scroll, except the bottom and the outside of B7-13 according to the diagram. Lay the B7-13 scroll on top of the B1-6 scroll, matching up the markings, and sew them together. Now glue down small outside edge of 12B. Lay the "A" scroll on top of the raw edge of the "B" scroll and sew them together.

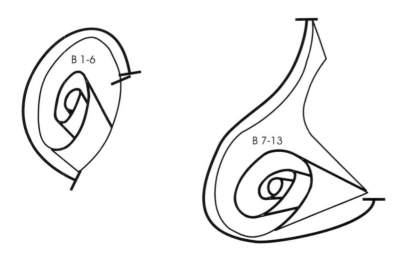

Step 3: The "C" Scroll. Sew the 1C-7C small half of the scroll. Sew the 8C-13C large half of the scroll. Glue the outside seam of the C1-7 scroll, except the bottom and the outside of C8-13, according to the diagram. Lay the C8-13 scroll on top of the C1-7 scroll, matching up the markings, and sew them together. Now finish gluing down all the outside edges.

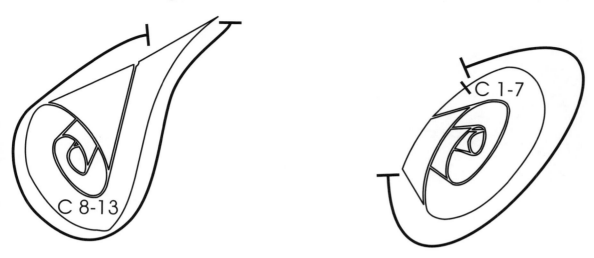

Step 4: The "E" Scroll. Sew the 1E-6E small half of the scroll. Sew the 7E-12E large half of the scroll. Glue the outside of the E1-6 scroll except the bottom and the outside edges of E7-12 scroll along the outside edge according to the diagram. Lay the big scroll on top of the small scroll, matching up the markings, and sew them together. Now glue down the small outside edge of 11E. Lay the "C" scroll on top of the raw edge of the "E" scroll and sew them together.

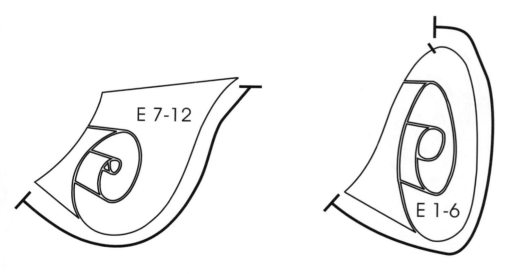

3-D Explosion

Step 5: The "D" Scroll. Sew the 1D-6D small half of the scroll. Sew the 7D-12D large half of the scroll. Glue the outside of the D1-6 scroll, except the bottom and the outside of D7-12, according to the diagram. Lay the D7-12 scroll on top D1-6 scroll, matching up the markings, and sew them together. Now glue down the small outside edge of 11D. Lay the "C/E" scroll group on top of the raw edge of the "D" scroll and sew them together.

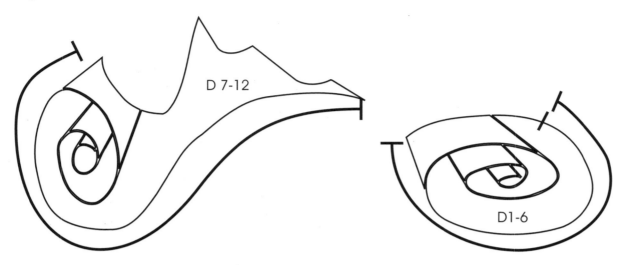

Step 6: The "F" Scroll. Sew the 1F-8F small half of the scroll. Sew the 9F-16F large half of the scroll. Glue the outside of the F1-8 scroll except the bottom and the outside of F9-16 scroll, according to the diagram. Lay the F9-16 scroll on top of the F1-8 scroll, matching up the markings, and sew them together. Now glue down small outside edge of 15F. Lay the "A/B" scroll unit on top of the raw edge of the "F" scroll and sew them together. Lay the "C/D/E" scroll unit on top of the raw edge of the "F" scroll and sew them together.

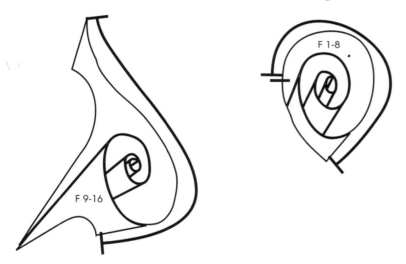

Step 7: Finishing: Now you have your complete appliqué. Huge, isn't it? I gave the monster appliqué 10" borders, so I cut my background a bit larger than the 110"X 87" measurement, quilted it, and cut it to size. Quilting can really change the shape of your top. Be sure to quilt it evenly all over. If you quilt it heavily like I do, you might find that wrinkles are less of a problem.

3-D Explosion

Quilting and Binding by Machine
(Why I don't have holes in my fingertips anymore)

I like thread very much. My quilts are quilted heavily because it's fun to do, looks great, and gives me an excuse to buy lots of thread. Heavy quilting seems to keep the worst of the wrinkles away as well, which is important to me, since my quilts live in and out of suitcases and travel all over the country with me.

At this writing, neon colors are my new best friends! The spools can be scary with so much neon wrapped together in one place. But once it is quilted onto a quilt, it will give the design that extra sparkle.

I match the color of the fabric I am quilting and free motion in the direction that the scroll rolls. You can see this clearly on the photograph of the Colossal Scrolls quilt. If you look closely at the quilt, you will notice that within each fabric area there is a very dark thread to create a shadow, a matching thread in the main body, and a third thread color to create a highlight. I have found that creating these shadows and highlights can be nice, but are not at all necessary to the 3-D illusion.

As for binding, let me tell you that I can be a very impatient person. By the time I put the binding on the quilt, I want it done so that I can go on to the next quilt.

Here is basically what I do :
- Measure my quilt all the way around, divide that measurement by 40" (width of fabric) for the number of strips and round up.
- Cut binding strips 2½" wide, join them together in a strip and press it in half, wrong sides together.
- Sew the binding onto the top of the quilt with the raw edge of the binding lined up with the raw edge of the quilt, mitering the corners as you go. Tuck in the ends using whatever method you prefer.
- Press your binding around to the back, mitering your miters on the back.
- Now, here is the trick. Get out your zipper foot. This foot stays to the left of the needle. The idea is to stitch on the top of your quilt again, right next to the folded binding and catching the binding folded underneath as you go, securing everything in place. I use a decorative thread to do this. I don't want anyone to think I was trying to sneak a fast one by, I want my work to look as if it is on purpose. Because it is!

If this description is not in depth enough for you, please pick up any basic quilting book and you will find a complete description of the process. I don't want to re-invent the wheel when there are so many good wheels out there already!

In closing, I hope you have enjoyed this book and you are inspired to make one of these projects or a quilt of your own design. I do answer email, so please visit my web site at www.doodlepress.com if you have a question. I also travel around the country to teach and lecture most of the year and I am available for bookings. Thank you!

Cara Gulati

Resources

These are some of my favorite suppliers of things that make my various jobs from quilter to publisher possible.

Sewing machines:
Bernina of America
3702 Prairie Lake Court
Aurora, IL 60504
630-978-2500
www.berninausa.com

Thread:
Superior Threads
PO Box 1672
St. George, UT 84771
(435) 652-1867
http://www.superiorthreads.com

Fusible Batting:
Hobbs Fibers
200 South Commerce Drive
Waco, Texas 76710
www.hobbsbondedfibers.com

Printing for self-publishers:
Tri-State Printing Co.
157 North Third Street
Steubenville, OH 43952
800-642-1166
www.tristateprintingco.com

Fabulous digital photography:
Gregory Case Photography
Gregory S. Case
415-112 N. Mary Ave., #358
Sunnyvale, CA 94086
(408) 248-9721
photos@gregorycase.com
www.gregorycase.com

For the best self-publishing classes and the woman who introduced the idea of glue into the appliqué process for me:
Beth Ferrier of
Applewood Farm Publications
3655 Midland Road
Midland MI 48603
989-799-6973
www.applewoodfarmquilts.com

Look for these fabric manufacturers in your favorite quilt store:
Timeless Treasures, Northcott, and Free Spirit Fabrics.

About the Author

Cara Gulati has been quilting since 1992. Little did she know that she was embarking on her future! She started her professional career by selling clothes in retail stores during college. She went on to design costumes and wedding gowns, eventually opening her own wholesale business designing and manufacturing children's clothes.

After that she decided that flat fabric creations were fun and to learn everything she could about quilting and fiber art. She began teaching quilting in 1999. Along the way she was designing her own quilts and thought it would be fun to publish a line of patterns, so Doodle Press (www.doodlepress.com) was born in 2002.

At the same time she began creating large art quilts in a series called 3-D Explosion. These quilts have helped her to create a niche. Her newest quilt in the series, 3-D Party Explosion, won Viewer's Choice at the Houston International Quilt Festival in 2003.

Now her full-time career involves lecturing and teaching nationally, publishing patterns and books, and creating giant art quilts. She has her office and studio her home, which is in a forest. It's great for taking breaks and walking with her dogs. Cara lives in Nicasio, in Marin County, California.

3-D Explosion

3-D Explosion

Simple Sammy Scroll
©2004 by Cara Gulati
www.doodlepress.com

WRONG SIDE
TEMPLATE PATTERN
ENLARGE 400%

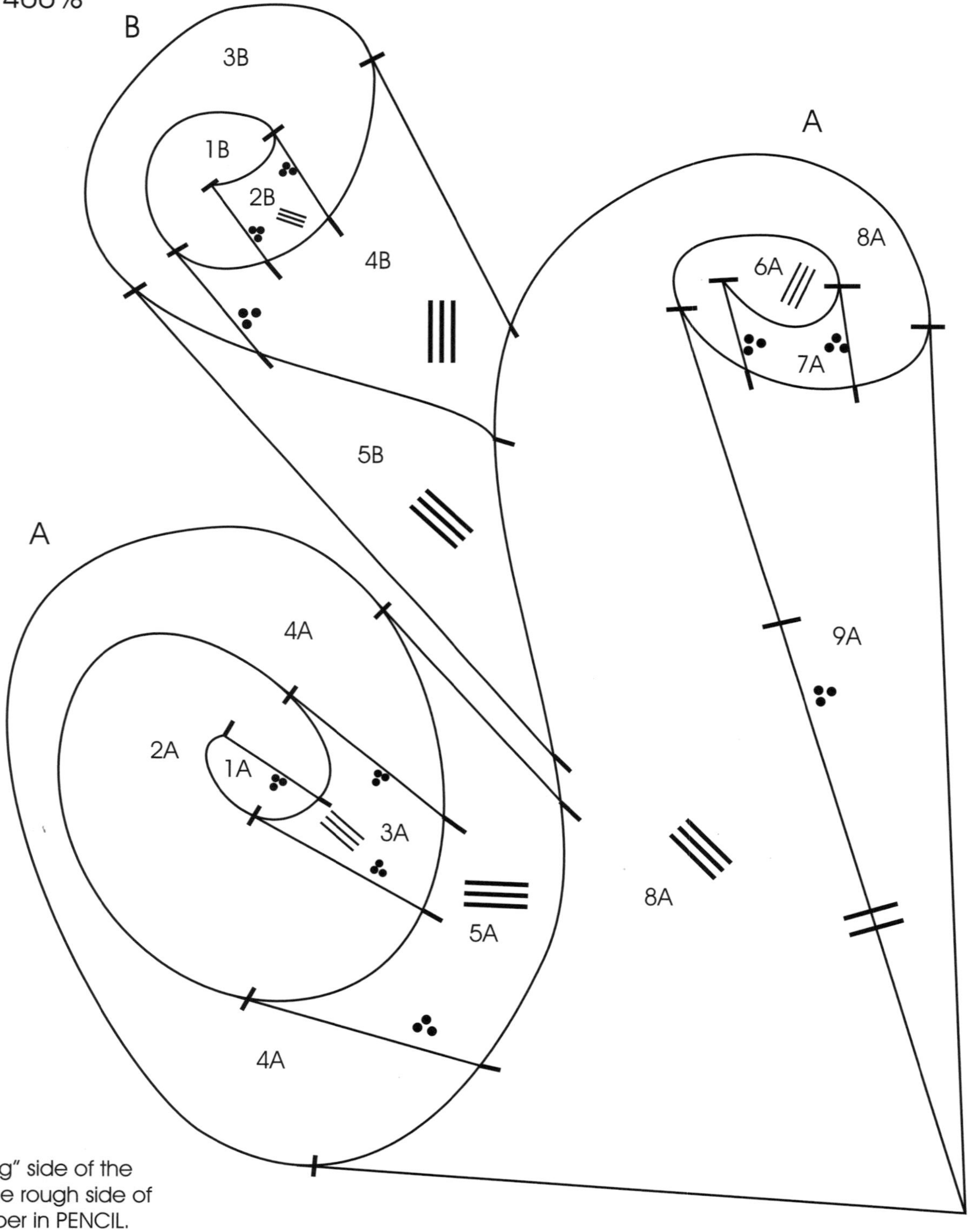

B

3B

1B

2B

4B

A

8A

6A

7A

5B

A

4A

2A

1A

3A

9A

5A

8A

4A

Copy this "wrong" side of the
drawing onto the rough side of
your freezer paper in PENCIL.
Transfer all markings.

See 3-D Explosion book for details.

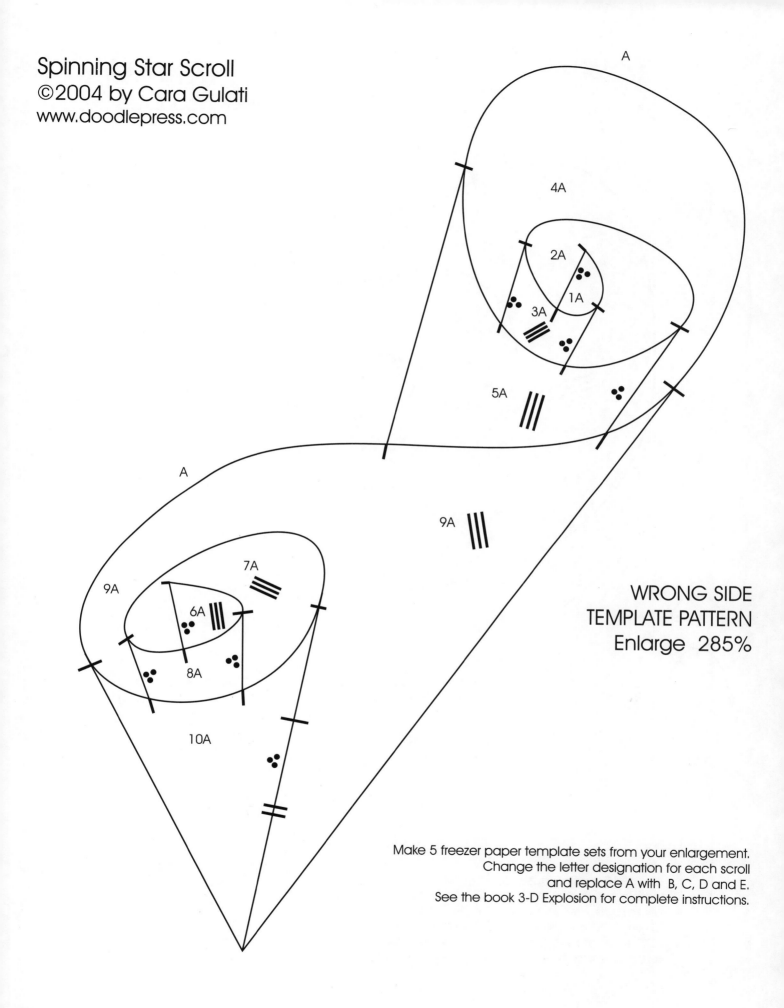

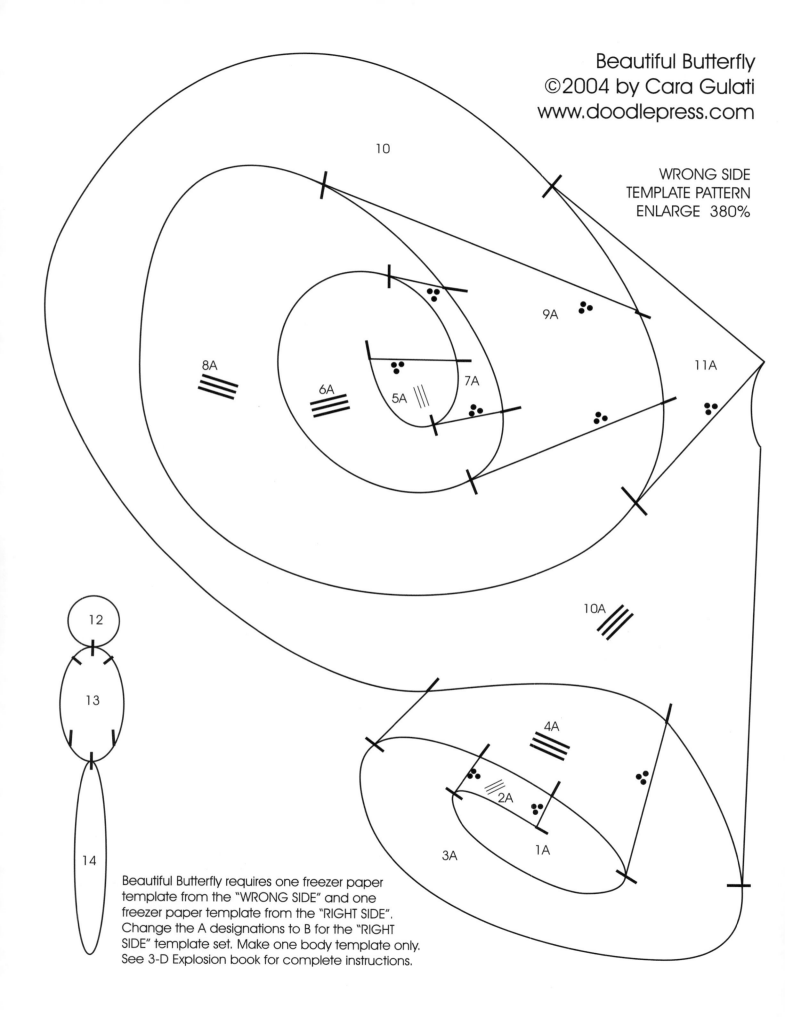

Reflections
© 2004 by Cara Gulati
www.doodlepress.com

WRONG SIDE
TEMPLATE PATTERN
ENLARGE 200%

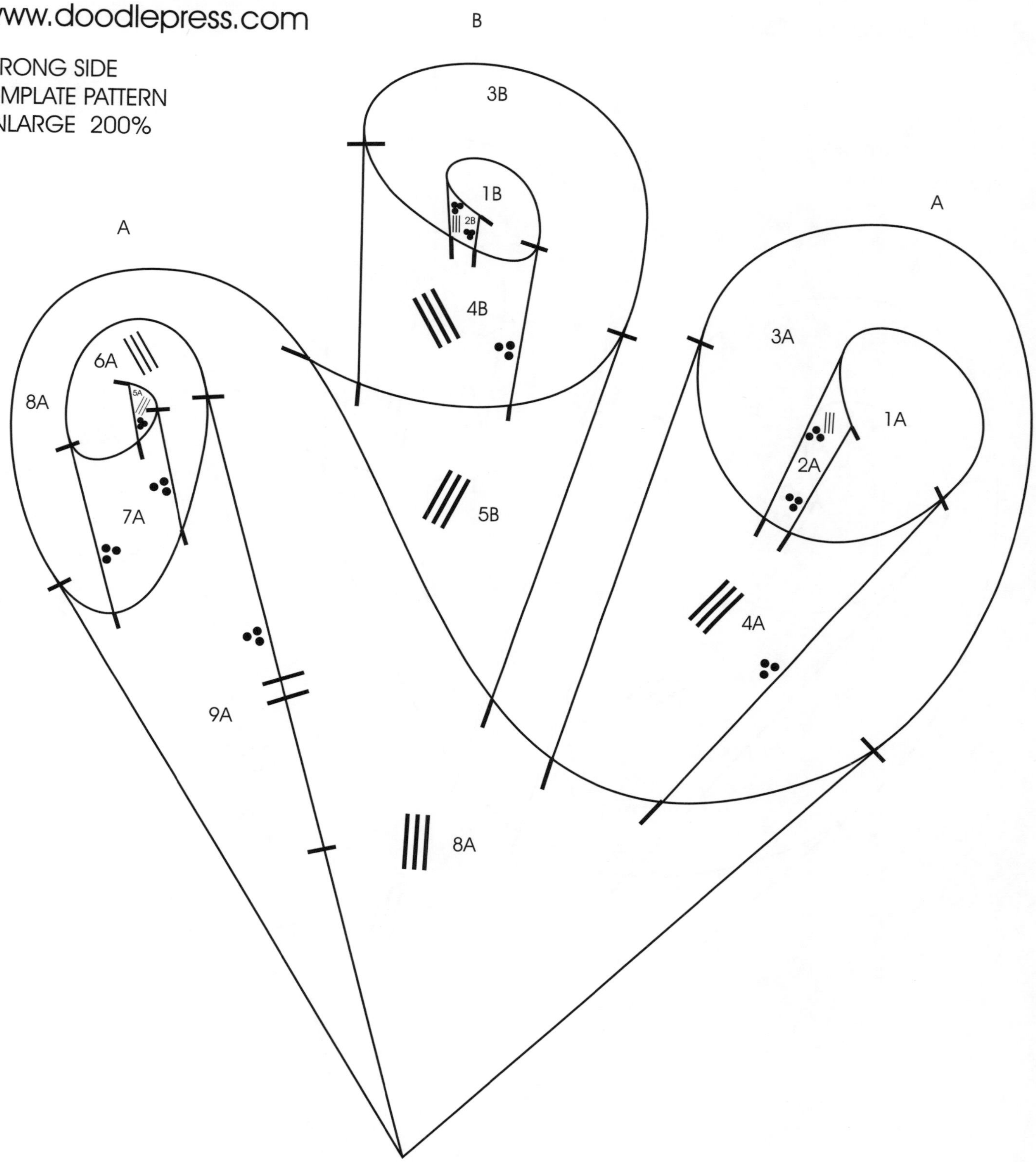

B

A

A

3B

1B

2B

4B

6A

8A

5A

7A

3A

1A

2A

5B

4A

9A

8A

Flower Reflections! requires 2 freezer paper
templates sets traced from the
WRONG SIDE and 2 freezer paper
template sets traced from the RIGHT SIDE
of your enlargement. Change the letter sets for each
template set, changing AB to CD, EF and GH. See book
3-D Explosion for further instructions.

Framed!
© 2004 by Cara Gulati
www.doodlepress.com

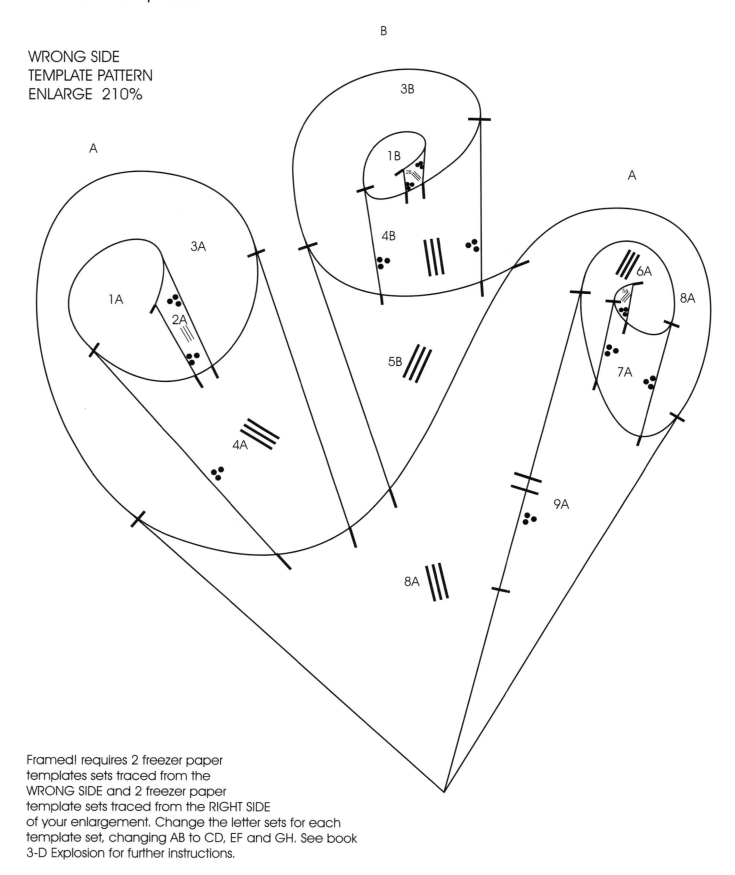

WRONG SIDE
TEMPLATE PATTERN
ENLARGE 210%

Framed! requires 2 freezer paper
templates sets traced from the
WRONG SIDE and 2 freezer paper
template sets traced from the RIGHT SIDE
of your enlargement. Change the letter sets for each
template set, changing AB to CD, EF and GH. See book
3-D Explosion for further instructions.

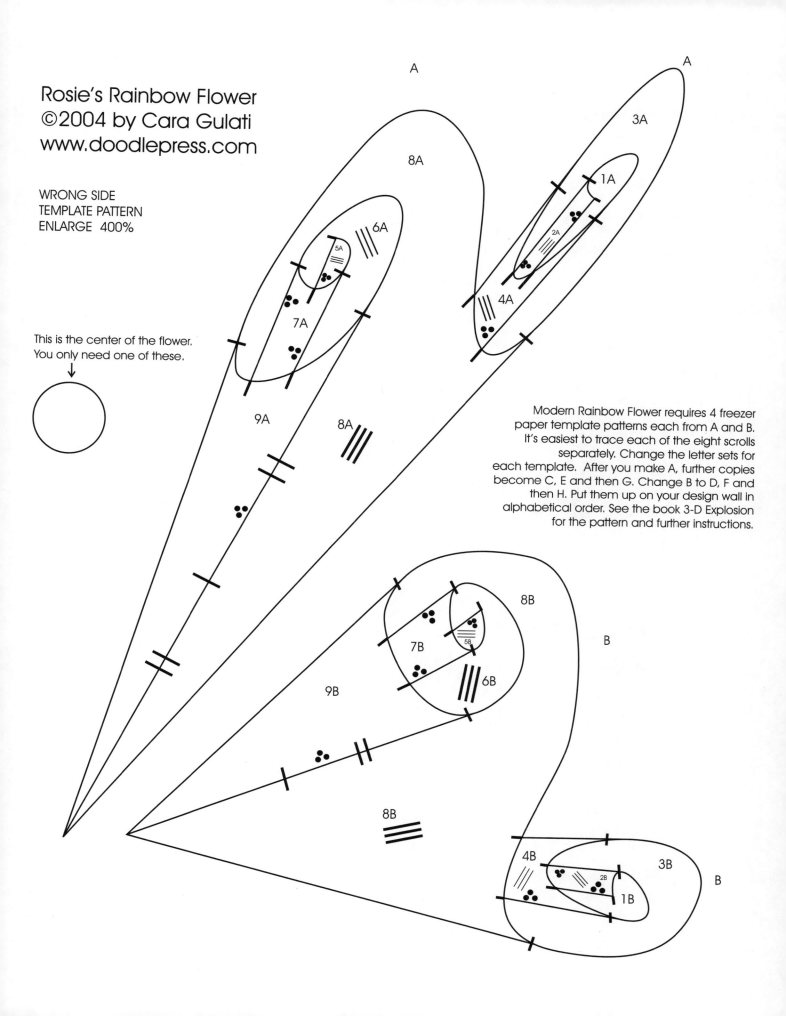

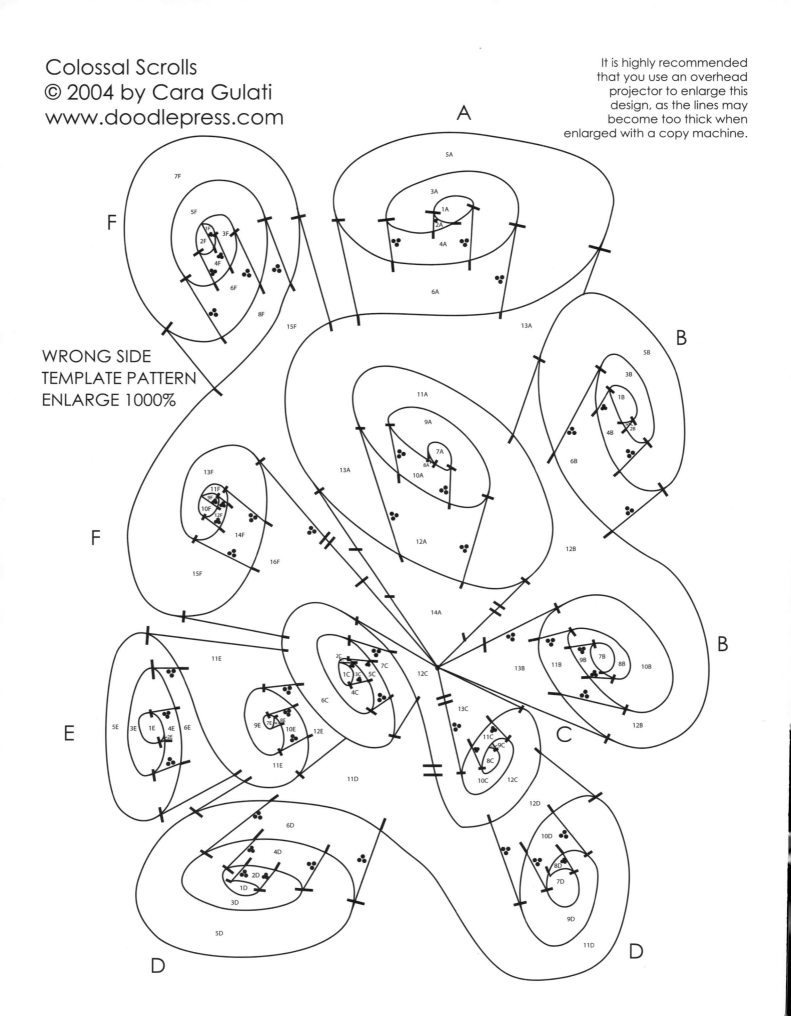

Simple Sammy Scroll
©2004 by Cara Gulati

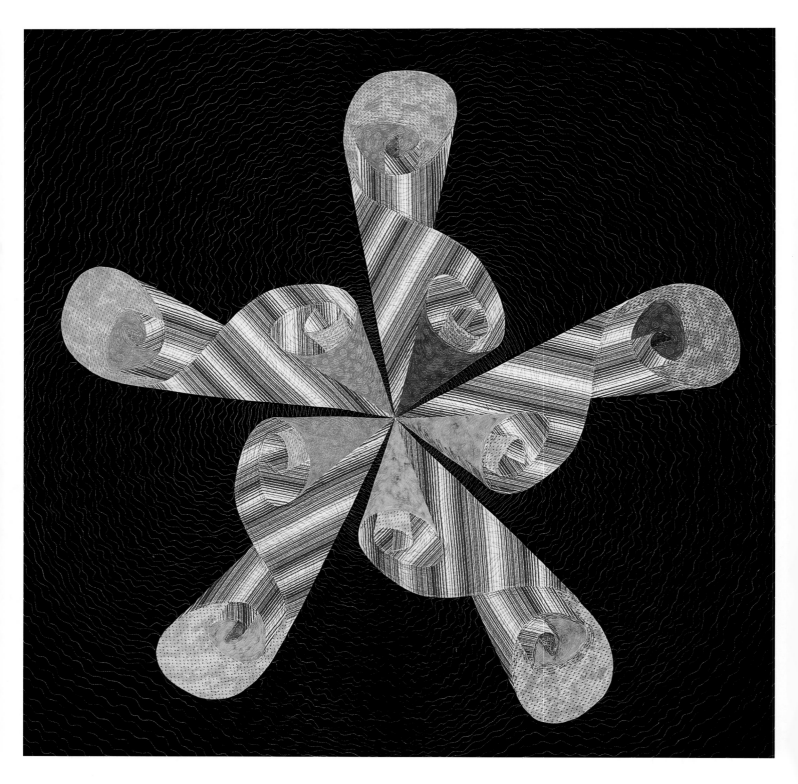

Spinning Star Scrolls
© 2004 by Cara Gulati

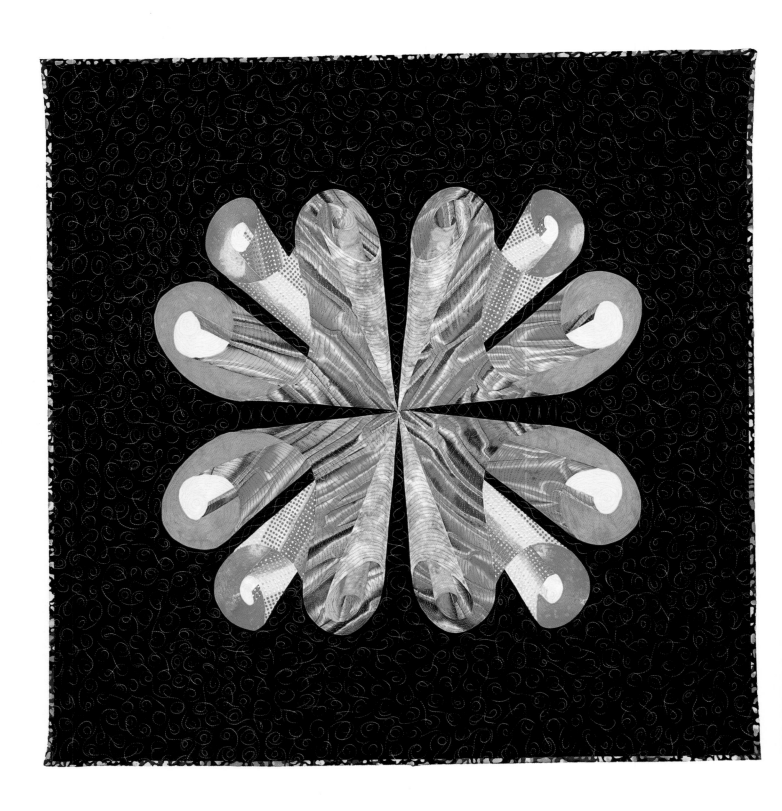

Reflections
© by Cara Gulati

Framed!
© 2004 by Cara Gulati

Rosie's Rainbow Flower
© 2004 by Cara Gulati

Colossal Scrolls © 2002 by Cara Gulati

3-D Party Explosion
© 2003 by Cara Gulati
This quilt is not a project in this book. It was the next in the 3-D series after the
Colossal Scrolls quilt. It also won Viewer's Choice at the Houston International Quilt
Festival in 2003. I am including it to give you some more ideas to play with! Have fun!